Dear Debbie

Shoot the Parrot,
Tame the Chimp
and Silence the Mouse

Love Krissie x .

Shoot the Parrot, Tame the Chimp and Silence the Mouse

How negativity, fear and doubt
get in the way of our riding and our life

Dr. Krissie Ivings

Written and Published by Aspire Therapy Services
© Copyright 2023
Print Edition

ISBN: 978-1-7395903-1-4

Design and Print by Printexpress (Buxton) Ltd
The Old Schoolhouse, Market Street, Buxton SK17 6LD

To the mare who no-one wanted, my gorgeous Ambers Echo.
You gave me wings.

Table of Contents

Introduction

If you had told the 16 or 18 year old me that one day I would write a book on sport psychology, rider confidence and peak performance, I would have laughed in your face. Almost nothing would have seemed less likely.

The brutal reality is that I am, in an athletic sense, entirely ordinary and wholly unremarkable. I am a few kilos on the wrong side of 'lean'. I run like a duck. I ride like a sack of potatoes. I am uncoordinated, clumsy and asymmetrical. I have no spatial awareness and poor proprioception. I have no natural ability whatsoever, in any sport. I was once kicked out of dance class for messing the routines up deliberately. I was actually trying my best.

I also had the fairly common baggage of 'not good enough' or 'what will people think', and the near universal blahness of 'can't be bothered' whenever the weather was bad, or I was feeling a bit tired or busy. Other people had motivation and self-belief. They were aspirational, confident, courageous and positive. They had energy and enthusiasm. And talent. Lucky them. I just had crazy fantasies while I nibbled hobnobs.

I love to read, and books are my immediate go to whenever I am facing any kind of challenge. As I slowly ventured more into the world of sport, I read sports books. Many, many sports book. I discovered that most of those books approach the subject by looking at what the top athletes are doing. Trying to elicit the secrets of these elite 'winners' on the assumption that if normal folk embrace the mindset and behaviours of those top performers, then we, too, can excel.

But in my view, those top performers are outliers. They are not like you and me. Frequently described are intensity and commitment evident from early childhood: 'Johnny ran 6 miles before and after school every day and always refused cake, even on his birthday'; 'Freddie picked up his first chess set aged 5 and by the time he was 7 he was playing 6 hours a day and beating all the teenagers at the local chess youth club' sort of thing. Perhaps some people have the 'obsessive focus while still at primary school' gene. But many of us have the 'can't be bothered if it's a bit drizzly' gene. Where is OUR book?

By definition, a vanishingly small number of people get to 'the top' in any sport. But most books on sporting success focus on that tiny group. I am never going to be 'successful' on any objective measure. Almost no amateur rider or athlete is. But success, to me, is achieving something new, improving, getting better, breaking through performance ceilings, overcoming self-limiting beliefs, setting and achieving goals that are huge for me and going further than I ever believed possible.

This book is for ordinary men and women with big dreams but a lack of innate motivation, lots of self-doubt and high levels of fear. Fear of danger, fear of failure, fear of looking like an idiot. This is a book about how to translate those dreams into reality. And how to change your mindset completely so that you can embrace your riding and your life fully.

While this book is mostly about riding it starts with endurance sport as this is where my personal transformation started. I developed better habits which affected my thoughts and feelings. Over time, my self-belief was able to grow. Riding is my current passion, but running and triathlon were the furnace in which I began to forge mental strength, resilience and a totally different mindset.

The book is set out in 4 parts:

In Chapter 1 we explore what our dreams, goals and plans actually are. Or could be. What do we want out of horse ownership and sport? What do we want to achieve? We are far more likely to get there if we know where 'there' actually is. This also explores intrinsic versus external motivation. What lights you up? What do you want to do? Is your riding life aligned with your true motivation and passion? This is crucial because so many people aren't at all sure about what they want, and are highly influenced by external factors and other people. This lack of clarity about your hopes, dreams and goals creates a lot of uncertainty, frustration and drift. This also means that you may commit to goals that you are not really invested in deep down. Or that you don't commit to goals you could be passionately invested in, because you have not clarified, in your own mind, what it is you actually want to do.

In Chapter 2 we discuss general lack of motivation or commitment. The procrastination and indecision that leads to us drifting in our goals and plans, putting things off for another day, season or year. The way in which we easily talk ourselves out of our intentions. The good news is that there are simple fixes for these issues. It's possible for even the most indecisive procrastinator to follow through with more consistency and more commitment.

In Chapters 3-8 we look at specific rider confidence problems represented by Chimp, Parrot and Mouse. These animals symbolise that critical inner voice and the nagging worries that give rise to fear, negativity and doubt. Not only do they make us scared to ride, they also eat into our enjoyment of our horses, and prevent us from accessing our skills when we need them most. These chapters aim to help you rediscover your love of horses, and of riding, by showing you how to subdue those pesky animals so you can ride with confidence, pull out peak performances in the heat of competition, and shift training blocks that may be impeding progress in whatever area you are working on.

The final chapters 9 and 10 expand on these themes to cover more universal ideas of how to be happy and successful, including how you actually define 'success'.

The book mainly focuses on horse-riding but also embraces universal ideas, suitable for all sports, and for life in general. Zen and the Art of Running, Riding & Living.

The phrase 'if I can do it anyone can' is horribly overused. But in my case it really is true. People like me don't run marathons and ultra-marathons. People like me don't do iron distance triathlons. People like me don't set and achieve major sporting goals. People like me don't go eventing. Only I did and I do. This book aims to help you reach your dreams too.

People Like Me

The book describes a transformation that initially started to take place entirely by accident. It could very easily never have happened at all, in which case I would still be the 'type of person' who makes and breaks goals, the 'type of person' who dreams but never plans, has no will power, no commitment. Still riddled with self-doubt, paralysed by fears and plagued by loss of motivation.

Apart from being reluctantly dragged to swimming lessons a few times a week, I never really did much sport as a child. I enjoyed PE but was pretty poor at it. I spent a couple of weeks after Wimbledon every year hitting foam balls against the wall of the house with my Junior Dunlop, dreaming of tennis triumphs, but these ambitions never even made it onto a court, let alone into competition. I was briefly inspired by Zola Budd at the Los Angeles Olympics to become a middle-distance runner. My 'training plan' to achieve this involved estimating how many laps of the house it took to run 1500m (about 40) and circling endlessly. I never went to a running club or track, and the brief spark of running enthusiasm withered before that autumn's blackberries did. I used to love watching show-jumping on the BBC with my grandmother, and regularly rode glorious clear rounds on the arm of the sofa. But jumping a real horse around a real course seemed like a totally impossible dream.

I was horse crazy from as early as I can remember but with absolutely no possibility of having my own pony. Instead, I had a life size poster on my bedroom door of a stable with a horse looking out, and I spent many hours riding my imaginary palomino pony. Despite my total lack of skill or opportunity, I still dreamed of playing at Wimbledon, running the London Marathon or riding at Badminton. Don't we all? I just knew nothing like that could ever realistically happen.

The world seemed to be divided into people who did cool stuff and people who watched other people doing cool stuff, while never believing anything like that could ever be possible for the likes of us.

I watched my first London Marathon at aged 15 in 1985. I gawped at the thousands of athletes of all shapes and sizes, as if gazing at exotic animals in a zoo. They were simply a breed apart. I remember thinking 'I'd love to do a marathon' but the thought never crystallised into any sort of intention or plan. People Like Me didn't do things like run marathons. I didn't even *know* anyone in real life who did things like run marathons. Simple as that.

But People Like Me still dream. Tennis courts are packed after Wimbledon, running participation surges after the London Marathon and participation in all sports was massively boosted by the 2012 Olympic Games in London. However, each year, as weeks go by, those initial bursts of enthusiasm and inspiration die away.

Like many people I launched many 'New Year/ New Me' campaigns. I joined gyms, I dieted, I ran, I swam. Just never for very long and never with any consistency.

And yet here I am 30 years on, looking back at many years of ultra-running, triathlon, and eventing. With no plans to stop any time soon. Still dreaming but now translating those dreams into reality. Doing things that once upon a time would have seemed as remote as the moon. And still do sometimes – but I do them anyway.

This is not the story of how I entered a Parkrun, discovered innate talent aged 24 and enjoyed a meteoric rise to make the Olympics a few years later. It's not that kind of book and I am very definitely not that kind of athlete. (Disclaimer – I have never (yet!!) won any affiliated competition. At any level.)

But the true beauty and joy of sport is that there is a thriving grass roots scene in every sport where newcomers are welcome and you can participate fully, no matter your level – complete beginner or one sponsor shy of professional. Sport grants you access to wonderfully inclusive communities. I have raced triathlons at the same time and over the same course as Olympic and World Champions and been overtaken by Junior World Champion, Jodie Swallow and Senior World Champion, Simon Lessing. I have completed multi-day mountain marathon races and 24 hour endurance events and been interviewed on the television. I was being interviewed as an also-ran, obviously, but I ran every inch of those trails, just like the winners.

People who decide it's not for the likes of us are generally self-excluding because of our own emotional baggage. We can change our thinking around this. We can do whatever we want. And do it with positivity, enthusiasm, commitment and pride. Every step further on from along from where we are right now is a legitimate success, deserving of celebration.

People Like Me..... can do whatever we want! Ordinary, wholly unremarkable people, people just like you and me, can do extraordinary and remarkable things.

Never Turn Your Hobby into a Job

I obeyed that rule for about 20 years. I am a Clinical Psychologist. Like so many people in the medical profession, I rarely applied the advice I gave others to my own life. However, I became aware through my athletic efforts that I had somehow developed mental toughness. I was far weaker physically than many people I ended up out-performing. I had also become happy to enter events with a real risk of ending dead last. Which I very often did, at least initially. I realised I had overcome a huge bout of imposter syndrome, as the idea of 'failing' in such a public way would once have horrified me. I realised I was now willing to 'Have A Go' as advised by BHS Fellow and renowned coach William Micklem in his 'Go Rules' for sporting success. Rule 1 being, simply: 'Have a Go' and rule 2 being: 'Have Another Go!'. A simple enough idea, but why do so many people self-exclude from taking that first step and giving something a go. Why did I?

Developing 'grit' and the willingness to just try had nothing to do with innate mental resilience. I avoided completely or gave up at the drop of a hat earlier in my life. This new willingness began to arise when I realized that I was teaching skills like positive reframing, supportive self-talk, mindfulness and attentional focus to help people overcome major depressive disorders, debilitating anxieties or suicidal urges. These skills and strategies readily transferred across to my own life, and I had instinctively started using them myself. They work!

I also had a phobic fear of jumping, born of long-term avoidance following a rotational fall in a cross-country riding lesson. I used my skills and knowledge from clinical psychology to deal with it effectively. That remains, and always will be, a work in progress and that is totally fine. If I do the work, my confidence stays high and I truly love jumping. If I have a blip, after a fall or a long gap, I know what I need to do to get back to that place of confidence. Bounce-back-ability is another skill.

These skills, like any other, need constant practice. They are as much a part of my riding development, as the schooling sessions and riding lessons. The therapeutic modalities in which I trained, and have worked for 30 years are Cognitive Behaviour Therapy or CBT and Dialectical Behaviour Therapy, or DBT. Neither have anything to do with lying on a couch and discussing dreams or childhoods, (apart from initially, to try and understand where some issues came from in the first place). Instead, we focus on actively changing thinking patterns and behaviours, then waiting for feelings to catch up. Which they always do. In this way, you can build the life you want.

Psychologists, like any other human beings, can be prone to self-doubt, anxiety, stress, negativity and depression. In fact, more so, in many ways because we have discovered that there is no hidden secret to protect against all of that. No Magic Therapy Fairy Dust we can sprinkle on clients or ourselves to erase mental distress. Many of us are attracted to this line of work in the first place because of personal experience of mental health issues. Imposter Syndrome is a huge problem for many therapists: we sit there hearing terrible stories of unrelenting distress and feel an overwhelming sense of responsibility, coupled with inadequacy, and think, 'well what are you telling ME for – go find a grown up!'

I was skilled at my job but my private life was a mess. I was anxious and depressed. I had Post Traumatic Stress Disorder (PTSD) following a life-threatening accident and didn't even know it. This came to light when I videoed a clinical session with a man who had developed PTSD after witnessing the murder of his friend. In the video I kept unconsciously referring to the murder as the 'ACCIDENT'. Until I saw it on-screen I had no idea I was using that word, which was the most appallingly inappropriate word to use in that context. I had not realized that I had the accident running through my mind on a more or less permanent basis, along with more acute flashbacks, hypervigilance, nightmares, an inability to sleep and depression.

I turned to mindfulness and other practices from the Buddhist tradition, alongside getting more traditional therapeutic support, and found that I benefitted more from blending Zen Mindfulness with CBT than either approach offered alone. I therefore started adopting these approaches in my NHS work too. This blend has since become completely established in therapeutic work. So much so, that mindfulness-based therapies are now described as the 3rd wave of psychotherapies after behavioural and cognitive approaches.

I had learned positive mental strategies, developed resilience and mental toughness, and embraced positive behaviours. All of these tactics broke down performance barriers, initially to participating at all, and later to happiness and success while participating. Then I started helping friends deal with their riding difficulties too, and realised just how rapidly people could over-come their fears, and regain confidence, with a bit of informed help.

My first client/friend had tried having lessons before she asked me for help. She could not even get on the horse without sobbing and hyperventilating, even at halt on a lead rein. She spent the first 30 minutes of our session telling me she was never going to ride again. She ended that first session happily trotting around the arena, off the lead rein, with a massive beaming smile on her face, shouting "KRISSIE I'M RIDING, I'M ACTU-ALLY RIDING!"

I had spent years trying to separate out the different aspects of my life, jumping into different streams at different times – the endurance athlete stream, the therapist stream, the riding stream, the horsemanship stream. But these streams were blending and combining in all sorts of unexpected ways:

I was using insights from horseman Mark Rashid to help depressed clients. I'd find myself explaining ideas highly relevant to overcoming mental distress from Rashid's book, *Life Lessons from a Ranch Horse.* (Though generally not letting the client know that the advice I was offering came from a quarter horse called Buck.)

I was using DBT skills designed to address suicidal behaviours to enhance athletic performances, predomi-nantly the Acceptance skills required to stay safe during moments of overwhelming distress. Which I had discovered are also very useful for staying peaceful, relaxed and accepting of the pain of running over mountains in the snow wearing inadequate clothing.

I was supporting exploited and abused children to gain confidence in protecting themselves, and enforcing personal boundaries, by teaching them to train horses in groundwork, and I was using both mindfulness thera-pies and CBT strategies to support my own horsemanship, health and happiness.

Eventually I accepted that there was simply no separation between me the psychologist, me the athlete, me the rider, the trainer, the confidence coach and me the human being trying to muddle my own way through life and be happy.

The final piece of the puzzle was passion. I was no longer keeping psychology/sport psychology out of my own life and sport but it was still not a job, rather an ever-more time consuming and absorbing hobby. I then started helping more friends, and was using my horses in therapy sessions. I was increasingly discussing insights from my riding life with my patients. And I realized that working with horses and riders was not turning my hobby into a job so much as turning my job into a hobby.

Finally, in 2020, I came home. 30 years after deciding that working with horses was a hopelessly impractical dream for a novice adult who had never owned a horse before, I set up my initial rider confidence camps and started operating commercially. Aspire Equestrian was born.

Although it's a bit clichéd, a different quote perfectly captures my feelings: "Do what you love and you'll never work a day in your life." I love my job. When I am on the cross-country course at a camp watching someone who 'would never jump again' flying around, linking fences in tears of joy and disbelief, I find it extraordinary that I am actually at work and being paid. It certainly doesn't feel like 'work'.

I hope you find this book inspiring and entertaining and that it can help you get to your dreams a little more quickly than it took me to get to mine. But there's no hurry. Wherever you are right now, is where you are. From there, anything is possible.

Dream Big.

Krissie Ivings

CHAPTER 1

What do I Actually Want to do?

Finding True Motivation

Goal setting is an important skill, even for those who might say 'I have no goals. I just want to enjoy my horse'. Guess what? Your goal is enjoying your horse. Are you doing that effectively? Are your behaviours aligned to that goal? Or do you put pressure on yourself to do more, ride in bad weather or meet the perceived expectations of other people?

It does not much matter which goals you choose, but it is very useful to have some, as this means you are more likely to follow through on things that you do actually want to do. The first step is identifying what motivates you. What do you want to get out of your relationships with your horse? What other fitness or lifestyle goals matter to you? Do you want to ride anymore? Or to have horses? Do you want *this* horse?

These are not simple questions, and pursuing the wrong goal is never likely to work very well. True motivation comes from within and tends to last. Flawed motivation, influenced by other people or a sense of what you 'should' do, doesn't.

'Choices' driven by anxiety, doubt, or internal pressures or expectations, are also not likely to be aligned with your true motivations and beliefs. Many people, with high levels of anxiety, express their doubts about whether they want to get back on at all. Ever. They strongly consider selling their horses, and just giving up. Of course, there is no obligation to ride or keep horses. For some people, there may come a time when riding and horse care simply no longer excites or inspires them enough to deal with the stress, cost and heartache that is part and parcel of horse ownership. Equally, many people only consider giving up because they feel anxious and reluctant to ride, sapping their enthusiasm and motivation. Once anxiety has been addressed, then all thoughts of selling evaporate, as the joy and love of this crazy, amazing sport flood back.

Take Sally, for example. Her horse developed a bad back, and bucked her off several times when mounting, shredding her confidence in him and in herself. She told me she was going to sell her horse, that she would never regain her trust him and could never imagine riding again. Within 1 session she was riding off the lead rein. Within a month she was trotting around and riding on her own. Within 3 months she was out hacking. 5 months after the first session she flew around a 7 mile farm ride and will now pop fences by herself. She describes being with him at the yard as her 'happy place', and she can't imagine life without him. Selling would have been a tragedy.

If you are not sure if you really want to ride at all anymore, then start there. What did you love most about riding? If you could be magically transported back to a place of confidence, would those joyful rides still appeal? If not, what has changed? If your riding dreams have to change due to illness, disability, age, responsibilities or financial realities, is there another way to fall back in love with riding and horses. If not, why not?

I have given up ultra-running because chronic injuries meant that I could no longer do the volume of training required to enter events that looked exciting enough to appeal to me. I am self-aware enough to know that, without the thrill of those challenges, I would not be interested enough to do the training. I therefore stopped, and took up another sport that does excite and inspire me. This was an entirely personal decision, not influenced by other people, negativity, or anxiety. However, if I had quit, despite still loving it, driven by thoughts such as: 'it's embarrassing to be so slow', that outcome would have been driven by doubt and self-consciousness. And I would have lost an activity that I could still have found pleasure and fulfilment in.

It is important to spend time really thinking about what you truly want. Whether you want horses at all. And if you do, what you want to do with them? This is your own unique Riding WHY, discussed in detail below.

If your goal is to enjoy summer hacking with your horse, then it makes sense that dark, cold, wet winter miles are unappealing. So why do them? Cut yourself some slack and focus on what you do enjoy. And wait for Spring.

If your goal is to event in March, then plot the road from November to March so there is a focus and a purpose to those winter rides, which then become mentally easier to cope with.

During the 'Endurance Years' my winters focused on long, slow distance training. That was only tolerable because my goals were absolutely clear. I always had a specific and very challenging target: The Jurassic Coastal Challenge, the Ironman, the Equinox 24 hour solo run or some other ultra-long distance event. I had a plan and total commitment to it. Take those races away and no way would I have gone out in the wind, snow, rain, sleet and mud to slog out a run or ride for no obvious reason.

Your Riding Why

Simon Sinek did a TED talk that has had over 58 million views on what he calls the 'Golden Circle' comprising WHY/HOW/WHAT.

He is talking about the corporate world and commercial success being predictable, based on this circle, but it applies equally to sport or to any other endeavour.

WHY: Mission/vision/belief
HOW: Strategy
WHAT: The day-to-day actions/ the outcomes. What companies/individuals actually do.

WHY?
Mission and Motivation

HOW?
Strategy

WHAT?
Day to day decisions

Most people operate from the outside in. Focusing mostly on the what of what they do. The technical stuff. The 'what should we do today' or 'how should we respond to this event that has just happened' level of thinking. They focus least on the 'fuzzy' inner circle.

Inspired leaders, successful companies and elite athletes tend to operate from the inside out. They have vision and belief, (their WHY), which informs their planning and strategy (their HOW). The day to day 'WHAT' stuff just flows creatively and naturally from that.

'WHAT' level thinking is processed by our rational, logical, language driven neo-cortex. The HOW and the WHY levels operate in our limbic brain, which is where emotion sits. Emotion is a much more powerful driver of behaviour than logic. Operating largely at the rational/logical WHAT level will make sustained commitment to a goal much harder than if we involve the emotional parts of our brain.

The WHY is what inspires you and lights you up. Having a clearly articulated personal WHY is a powerful driver of behaviour and helps you create a strategy, a framework, an overall structure which forms your HOW. This HOW makes all your efforts more focused and purposeful. The WHAT then flows naturally from WHY and HOW, in a way that strongly aligns with your goals and values.

Simek discusses how most people use OUTSIDE IN thinking. Most attention stays at the 'what am I doing today' level, with less of it spent on overall strategy, and even less on linking activity to clearly understood motivations and goals. Whereas progress and success are far more linked to INSIDE OUT thinking.

KEY CONCEPT:
Focus on WHY and HOW, not just on WHAT

A very similar idea is expressed by Robert Dilts with his 'Dilts Pyramid', and is used frequently in Neuro Linguistic Programming (NLP). Dilts explains that most people work TOP DOWN, spending most time operating at levels, 1 and 2 and the least time at levels 5 and 6. Whereas BOTTOM UP thinking is much more effective.

Dilts describes the 6 levels as:

1) Environment

The external conditions and what other people did or did not do. The 'story' about what happened and why it happened. Generally speaking, this 'story' will not centre on the individual themselves and will not really hold them accountable or responsible for their own choices. Rather, the energy will be in explaining the external circumstances that led to a person's choices or behaviours. 'I was prepared to go but then Susan said she wasn't coming anymore, and I was not sure of the way, and anyway the weather forecast was rubbish, and I did not want to travel alone, and the horse was muddy and, and, and, and'.....

2) Behaviour

A person's immediate reactions to events around them. 'I didn't sleep well and I just wasn't really feeling it. Then as I was leading him from the field he seemed a bit on his toes which sent my anxiety up, so I thought forget it, I'm not riding today. Just not worth it.' There is a little more personal accountability here, but the individual remains highly reactive to external events.

Environment and behaviour equate to the WHAT level of the Golden Circle. Most people operate here:

I did this (behaviour) because of this (environmental factor or emotional reaction).

The weather was bad so I cancelled my lesson; my horse was on his toes so I decided not to hack; I couldn't find my bridle numbers so I withdrew from my dressage competition; I was not sure where the adaptor for the trailer electrics was and I did not want to travel to the yard and then not even be able to go.

At these levels we are reactive to external events and are easily swayed from course. We may try to influence our environment, but we are also heavily influenced by external factors, many of which are not under our control.

3) Capability or competence

This 3rd level relates to the HOW level of the Golden Circle. There is more of a focus on capability and competence, which drives behaviour through strategy, skills development, and forward planning. For example, you may recognise skills gaps and develop a plan to fill them. People operating at this level are more structured and focused than those only looking at day to day 'What' issues.

4) Belief

This is a person's underlying values, the core reasons driving behaviours.

5) Identity

This is your sense of self: your passions, motivations, what lights you up. What makes you tick.

6) Spirituality

This refers to your 'wisdom' mind. The deepest levels of personal truth.

The WHY of the Golden Circle is reflected in the Belief, Identity and Spirituality levels in the Dilts framework. This can be considered your Vision, Mission or Self-concept. Understanding your personal WHY helps you identify your intrinsic motivation: Do I actually want to do this? Why?

All levels become more effective when you use Bottom Up or Inside Out thinking or planning. The WHY powerfully influences the HOW, which then powerfully influences the WHAT. This is because the WHY levels are emotionally driven, and emotions are extremely influential in terms of what we end up doing.

If you don't consciously develop a vision or mission, and a self-concept, your brain will fill in the gaps and it will generally focus on extrinsic factors or surface level emotions. For example, anxiety leading to the thought 'I don't like competing', and that being simply accepted as 'true' when in fact the anxiety could easily just be centred in fear of failure, other people's expectations and your own unexamined beliefs.

Other people's priorities also become unhelpfully influential if you don't have a clear view of your own motivation and values.

For example, you compete because you think you 'should', you ride in winter because you feel guilty for being 'lazy' if you don't, you jump because your horse is a good jumper and you feel you will be 'wasting' his talents if you stick to hacking.

Riders generally focus mostly on the WHAT, maybe with a bit of strategy such as a training plan or some goals and a very cursory and unexamined WHY. That sort of outside in thinking and planning might look something like this in practice:

WHAT: School and hack and pop some jumps when feeling brave enough.

HOW: Fairly regular flat lessons, short hacks in company, jump lessons every few weeks.

WHY: To overcome nerves and get better at riding.

This is how I rode for years. But how effective is it?

Likely Outcomes

You are likely to do things you enjoy when schooling, rather than working on the areas that you find harder, which are the areas that are therefore limiting your progress. You may become frustrated by mistakes and therefore fall into the trap of repeating things you find easier. You may be reluctant to spend too much time in that uncomfortable place at the edge of your ability when you can't quite get something.

Your session may be unstructured and you may find that you drift from one issue to another. For example, you decide to practice transitions. You notice your horse is falling in so you start working on that. He finds it hard and comes above the bit so you deal with that, and so on. The session lacks focus, and little progress is made in any area, as you keep getting side-tracked from one issue to another.

When out hacking, you are likely to stay firmly in your comfort zone. For example, regularly repeating a particular loop with a trusted partner, reluctant to venture further afield.

If you are nervous about jumping you are likely to experience reluctance, and may tend to avoid jumping sessions. This results in too long a gap between lessons, and so you never really feel less anxious.

Even elite athletes can fall victim to a 'What' mindset. Middle distance runner, Jake Wightman, won gold in the 1500 metres at the 2022 World Championships. Afterwards, he described his bitter disappointment at finishing 10th in the 2020 Olympics in Tokyo. He explained that Tokyo made him realise he had to stop training in the ways he enjoyed and start doing the 'stuff I didn't like because I wasn't very good at it.'

His WHY was medalling at a major Championship, but his training had not been underpinned by that priority. After Tokyo, Wightman changed everything about how he trained, with single minded determination to align his training to his mission and vision. He then pursued this with full commitment, and achieved his dream.

Within the 'What' framework, a person is mostly focused on day-to-day decision making. Decisions are heavily influenced by Environment/Behaviour levels, which are generally outside of your control. Typically, the response to a problem, such as an incident on a hack, or a fall in a lesson, is despondency or frustration. People are easily discouraged, fearful and tend to have a 'back to square one' mentality if things go wrong. When you focus on issues arising day-to-day, and deciding what to do on the fly, problems seem disproportionately significant. On the other hand, if you plan and process events more holistically, within an overall strategy, working towards a clear vision, then those same problems are just seen as blips along the way. They are more likely to be viewed in context, and with more perspective. They can therefore be perceived and addressed in a more helpful, less catastrophic way.

Successful athletes, entrepreneurs or leaders take their WHY seriously. They have a clear MISSION and a clear VISION and work to cultivate a positive self-concept. That leads to effective planning and preparation, within an overall strategy.

> **KEY CONCEPT:**
> **If you don't find your own intrinsic motivation your behaviour will be strongly influenced by 'shoulds', external factors and other people**

Values and Goals Exercise

Putting your mission, vision and self-concept together creates your personal riding culture. Take plenty of time over this exercise to ensure you are riding and interacting with your horse in ways that are aligned to your goals and values.

MISSION/MOTIVATION

A) To improve myself and my horse and compete to our true potential
   Or
B) To develop a partnership so we can go anywhere/do anything and go on hacking adventures.
   Or
C) To enjoy my riding and my horse
   Or

D) To explore natural horsemanship and achieve the deepest possible connection with my horse, and ever-increasing lightness and softness.

E) ....

F) ....

VISION

A) Riding in harmony with confidence and skill on the flat and over jumps

Or

B) Cantering though woods, meandering by rivers, exploring the countryside together with freedom and joy

Or

C) Loving the horsey lifestyle. Doing a bit of everything with no pressure. Embracing my leisure/downtime with enthusiasm

Or

D) Cantering across a field, bareback and bridleless, in perfect harmony and attunement

E) ...

F) ...

SELF-CONCEPT

A) Committed to learning, willing to struggle by working on limiters, open minded, creative, flexible. Focused and willing to do the work needed consistently.

Or

B) Adventurous, nature loving, independent, free, enthusiastic

Or

C) Easy going, no pressure, loving life, riding when I want to, leaving it when I don't. Embracing all aspect of horse ownership including grooming, social aspects of being on the yard etc.

Or

D) Lifelong student of the horse. Endlessly reading, attending demos, experimenting, exploring and learning with curiosity.

E) ...

F) ...

The above is your personal riding culture.
This can help you develop:

- A more consistent schedule of lessons or riding activities
- A positive attitude to 'failure'
- More enthusiasm to seek out opportunities
- A more adventurous attitude
- Greater commitment to making things happen
- Less influenced by environmental factors
- A clearer and more progressive training plan
- Clarity over what you do and don't want to do so your riding is aligned to your values and goals and not to external expectations or pressures.

- Clearer boundaries about what you will and won't do as you are guided by intrinsic values and motivations.
- Greater curiosity and an open, enquiring mind.

Clarity about WHY helps you to clarify what you think and feel. And to own your values and wishes with confidence. Instead of feeling guilty for riding infrequently in winter, you can confidently say, 'oh I can't be doing with that mud malarkey. I'll ride in Spring.'

Instead of feeling under pressure to compete you can feel empowered to say 'I prefer the satisfaction of progressing in training without pressure.' Or 'competing is just not for me, far too much faff. I like the simplicity of me and my horse exploring the countryside together.'

Conversely, if you feel judged *for* competing, you can disregard anyone else's view, knowing you compete for your own satisfaction because that is what you find most inspiring or fulfilling. For example, when people say or write that BE80/90 isn't 'real' eventing anyway, you should train until you are capable of doing it 'properly', a clear WHY, centred on the love of competition, helps you to avoid feeling like a fraud, or feeling embarrassed by being at grassroots.

All my sporting life there have been people telling me I don't belong. 'Why do a marathon at all if you can't do it in sub 5 hours? That's just walking.' 'Why do an Ironman if you are just chasing cut off times? Ironman does not count until you are at sub 12 hours.' 'Eventing was better when Novice was the entry level. Then it meant something.'

Frankly, whatever you do in life, there will be people with an opinion about it. While being open to different perspectives is healthy, the route to riding in a way that is aligned to your own values and beliefs is to clearly know what those values and beliefs are. This helps protect you from being unduly influenced by other people's views, and ensures you are pursuing goals and dreams that are authentic and meaningful for you.

This attitude is exemplified by the wonderfully talented horseman, Joe Midgley. He did not learn to ride until he was 14, but rapidly decided he wanted to make a career out of training and riding horses. He came to that realisation while sitting in a classroom thinking, 'I just do not want to be here', and went out to make his dreams come true. At that stage, he lacked the skill and experience to charge anything at all for riding horses, let alone make a living from it. Undeterred, he rode and trained them for free, and soaked up knowledge, skills and experience however, wherever and whenever he could.

He also rapidly developed a values base and ethos centred on building a relationship with a willing partner, via effective communication. Rather than expecting horses to speak our language, he wants to understand theirs. Joe pursues this path with single minded dedication, totally unfazed by criticism from others who are on a different journey.

KEY CONCEPT:
Find your own motivation, own it and find
people who share it.

Clarity about the WHY also helps you question more superficial beliefs, and to overcome surface level emotion.

I don't like riding in the rain.
Why not?
It's wet and cold
So what?
It's not very nice?
How do you know?
Well it's obvious.
Have you ever ridden in the rain?
Yes.
How was it?
Actually alright once I got going.

In that example it was the thought of riding in the rain not the reality of it. But this unexamined thought means they are likely to simply give up whenever conditions are not perfect. A clearer focus on higher levels helps avoid that.

I overcame 'bad weather reluctance' with the simple mantra: 'If they will teach in it, I can ride in it'. This simple phrase transformed my perceptions, as my 1 hour in the rain paled into insignificance compared to the instructor's 6 hours.

Another example is:

I should compete.
Why?
People judge me if I don't
So?
I just don't like feeling judged.

In that example, the issue is fear of judgement and has nothing really to do with competing. How would that person feel if people judged you *for* competing, for example saying 'eventing is cruel. Who asked horses if they were happy to put themselves at risk like that?' If your behaviour would change with changing external perceptions, then it is under extrinsic motivation, which is far less powerful than intrinsic motivation.

I personally love to compete and I'd compete in secret if people had a problem with it, rather than give it up. In fact, I more or less have. During a heat wave in 2022 there was an event on a day that the temperatures were due to hit around 30 degrees. Both BE and FEI had said eventing in those temperatures were within their safety limits, but people needed to assess their own horse. My horse never showed any signs of struggling in the heat, plus the venue was local and my class was early: I was scheduled for dressage at around 8am, and due to be finished completely before 10, when temperatures were forecast to still be around 18 degrees. I took her and we had a great run. But there was a huge social media pile-on directed at anyone who evented that weekend, so I kept fairly quiet about it. I was totally comfortable in my decision, but I knew posting about it could attract criticism, or even abuse by people who did not know the full situation, or the reasons the risks were low for me and my horse that day. But it did crystallise for me that I am most definitely not eventing to prove anything to anyone else.

Everyone needs to work out their own motivation, their own riding WHY. Then use your clear sense of mission/motivation to help you plan a strategy, which is your HOW. Your WHAT logically flows from those. I would strongly recommend you look up Simek's TED Talk which goes into the Golden Circle in more detail, in an entertaining and accessible way. You can apply it to any sport or any work situation. I use it all the time and it has been life changing.

If you are operating from the Environment/Behaviour level, it is very easy to be put off by external events, and readily deflected by minor inconveniences or barriers. If you are driven by a strong WHY, then you are likely to have a dogged 'Make It Happen' mindset, and will be far better at adapting to external events. The day I was taking my horse, Lottie, to our first ODE, I was driving a new car and towing a trailer. The car went into limp mode 10 hilly miles from the venue. This could have been game over for the event. But as long as there was a way we could keep moving forward then that is what I planned to do. We phoned for rescue. The chap who came could not get the car out of limp mode, then said we needed to be low-loaded home. But it would be safer to get to the event and wait there where Lottie could be safely unloaded and graze, have access to water and so on. He gave us an escort to the venue, which we limped along to at around 5 mph.

I had every excuse to pull out: I was going to be late, I would not have time to walk the cross-country course properly, and trying to ride blind seemed ridiculous, plus I needed to sort out getting Lottie home as I had not realised my rescue package did not include horse transport. But I didn't. I decided to just focus on getting there and completing each phase as best I could. And only then to worry about figuring out how to get us all home again. I rang ahead to let the event secretary know what was happening, and was told I could go last in the class, as long as I was there before the next class started. I still had very little time, but as long as there was still a chance, then I was going to try to ride.

When we got there, I made it to dressage last and then barely made it to show-jumping. They were calling my number as I arrived and I had not walked the course yet. I watched the last but one rider jump, then warmed up for about a minute (luckily having trotted over straight from dressage so she was more or less warmed up anyway), went in and somehow jumped clear and – more surprisingly – with no errors of course. I had a small amount of time to try and figure out the cross-country, but not nearly enough, so I said to my friend that there was no way I could get round, especially as navigation is something I am really, really bad at. But I was going to try anyway and, to my astonishment and delight, the track I was jumping was the only one that had been ridden so far that day. The ground was wet and cut up, with a lovely, clear brown line all around the cross-country track showing me the way. Against all odds, the event was completed. In fact I was double-clear and got two precious qualifying points for a championship series I was participating in. And yet it would have been so, so easy to decide that it was simply not going to happen for me that day, and to give up before I'd even started.

> **KEY CONCEPT:**
> Have a 'make it happen' mindset. Sometimes you simply can't overcome barriers that get unexpectedly thrown in your way, but very often we give up because we 'won't be able to' not because we genuinely can't.

Summary

Goal setting is a complex skill, and it can be hard to work out what you genuinely want to do. Many people's 'goals' are externally driven, or are influenced by fear, doubt or the pressure they put on themselves. Riders often perceive vague reluctance or anxiety as evidence that they don't want to do it anymore. This can be very unreliable, and lead you to make decisions you deeply regret.

At the superficial What levels, folk find themselves heavily influenced by external factors or moment-to-moment thoughts and ideas. It is far more satisfying, and leads to far greater success, to identify your own personal Why, and to understand your intrinsic motivation. It is then also important to keep these insights at the forefront of your mind, and to use this self-awareness to guide your decisions and actions.

Once you know what you truly want, then the next step is stacking the deck in your favour, so you are more likely to reach those dreams and goals. There are a number of deceptively simple, but very powerful strategies, that can dramatically increase the likelihood that you will maintain consistency, stay focused and move forwards. Those simple steps turned me from a 'nice idea, but never gonna happen' dreamer, to someone who has actually followed through on increasingly ambitious challenges. These approaches are described in Chapter 2.

CHAPTER 2

How Did I Get Here?

The Endurance Years

When and what changed? When did I discover that motivation, aspirational thinking, confidence, positivity, energy, commitment, enthusiasm and grit are skills to **learn** and **earn**, not gifts from the angels granted at birth? And that all of these are more important for long term success than 'talent'.

With any significant change, the hardest part is starting. Taking those first few steps. And then setting the conditions for carrying on. This happened for me by chance. But understanding why and how things shifted in my thoughts, beliefs, attitudes and behaviours means you can create this deliberately, rather than waiting for fate to lend a hand.

The first turning point came when I joined the 'Ladies Social Joggers' at the local sport centre in Nuneaton. The title attracted me as it was reassuringly non hardcore. I found out later that some of the Social Jogging Ladies were highly accomplished athletes training for sub-silly marathon times and suchlike. But I was spot on in my assessment of the tone of the club. Welcoming, accepting, willing to help out duck-footed runner wannabees like me. There were various groups you could join. For total beginners you could walk/run around the football pitch. If you were slightly fitter you could do laps round the block, each lap being ¼ of a mile. But most of the runners would go out on A Road Run, (which was definitely worthy of capitalisation in my mind), the shortest of which was about 2 miles.

My first concrete, clear, meaningful, achievable goal was born. I wanted to make it out onto A Road Run. The football pitch/round the block runs were challenging enough (for me) to feel satisfying, and yet were easy enough to commit to each week. For the first time in my life I abandoned fantasy, ditching lofty goals with no plans in favour of something I could actually do. I could (literally) see the steps I needed to take. And for the first time, I developed some consistency. 6 short weeks after my first stumbling laps of the football pitch I ran 2 miles on the road. Sure, I had to walk/run the last half mile but I was ecstatic. I had gone on a proper, bona fide Road Run. I was a RUNNER! Go, me.

I certainly did not set my running goal with SMART goals in mind but the reality is that the goal was truly SMART. It was a **S**pecific, personally **M**eaningful, **A**spirational but **R**ealistic goal that could be achieved in a fairly short period of **T**ime.

The concept of SMART is hardly new. But like many clichés from the corporate world, there is something very powerful at its heart. How many of us actually apply SMART goals to ordinary life? We may do it on team building or management courses. But we don't do it in the areas that really matter to us. Which is kind of the wrong way round.

KEY CONCEPT:
Dream big but start SMALL. Choose
SMART goals

The other important elements for me were a concrete commitment which I told others about, and a club which supported my goal and told me what to do every week. I now know that this helps in many ways, chiefly reducing cognitive stress and increasing accountability.

Neuro-science tells us that all forms of mental stress are cumulative. Decision making takes up mental energy. So does finding your running gear. So does indecision about what to do. So does motivating yourself to get out of the door. If you have spent a lot of energy trying to decide what to do, you may not have enough mental resilience left to actually go and do it.

I had eliminated many of those additional demands on my brain, leaving enough capacity just to get the gear on and head out to the club. This is the reason why keeping a diary of what you intend to do, or following a plan from a book or magazine is so useful. For the same reason, meal replacement diets can be easier to stick to than ones in which you have to choose what and when to eat. All the decision making is done for you – you just need to follow the plan.

KEY CONCEPT:
Reduce decision making stress

Later still, I learned to even avoid the 'finding my stuff' stress. It sounds too simple to really work, but if the gym bag is packed the night before, the chances of lobbing it into the car to go running on the way home after work are very considerably increased. Similarly, if you plan to join an online Equipilates class at 7am, have the exercise mat and your gear next to your bed before you go to sleep. If you want to hack out before work, lay out your riding kit, and make sure you know exactly where everything you need is, so that you are not faffing about looking for Hi Vis or gloves or a head torch. Just the thought 'I'm not sure where I left my Hi Vis or whether my battery is charged' can be enough to keep you in your bed, your goal abandoned.

KEY CONCEPT:
Prepare for sessions in advance

Behaviour change is more likely to happen if we publicly commit to it. Patients who write down their next appointment date themselves are more likely to attend, than those who have the date written for them.

Communicating your plans to others helps makes you accountable. Get entered into an event and tell people what you've entered. Log progress on social media or Strava. Find a group or club to join. Accountability makes a huge difference to success.

KEY CONCEPT:
Make yourself accountable.

In 2022, the comedian, Jason Manford, posted the following on social media:

'Can some psychologist tell me how I am not able to motivate myself to do – say – 6 X 20 minute runs over 10 days but can do a 2 hour panic run at midnight on the last day of the month to collect some arbitrary points… And I'm finally on Bronze….. Feeling proud. Broken but proud.'

Yes, Jason, I can! Getting the points by the end of the month was SMART. Specific, clearly meaningful to Jason, aspirational but realistically achievable in a reasonably short space of time. He had reduced decision making stress by being signed up to a programme, which meant his workouts were set. He just had to do them. He was accountable because he was telling others about it online. He increased his levels of support by posting publicly, which resulted in a lot of positive comments and encouragement. Having people around you rooting for you, and celebrating your achievements, is also important. Those factors were enough to get him to put in the mammoth effort of a 2 hour run at mid-night on the last day, because the clearly defined and articulated goal depended on that.

His only problem was not planning and preparing which meant he did not reduce the cognitive stress that comes from just winging it. If you think 'I'll squeeze it in somehow', that takes up too much mental energy and it gets put off and off and off till you are out of time. As he discovered.

If you feel as though your goals are not supported and celebrated by those around you, find new people to surround yourself with. The vast majority of sports clubs or groups like Riding Clubs will happily cater to newcomers and beginners, but if you find one that doesn't, find another club or group.

There are also plenty of online options and plenty of forums that can be a place where you find like-minded people, from Tritalk to Horse and Hound Forum to breed society groups and Facebook groups promoting a particular philosophy or training approach. Some are awful, some are great. But dig around and there will be somewhere you feel you belong and are supported.

KEY CONCEPT:
Find a welcoming group and trust that they
want you there. They do! Honestly.

It is no surprise that there has been an explosion of participation in running as a result of initiatives like

Parkrun and Couch to 5K. Whether by accident or design, both Parkrun and Couch to 5K (and, in particular, Couch to 5k that leads you to Parkrun) use all the above strategies, which nudge you in the direction of achieving the goals you set.

Parkrun started in 2004 with 13 runners. There are now over 5 million people registered worldwide. In 2018 there were over a quarter of a million participants taking part every week. Research into the phenomenal success of this initiative, shows that many Parkrunners never ran before they started taking part in these welcoming events. Walkers, older adults, women, overweight people and people with disabilities are all very well represented at Parkrun.

The goal of completing a Parkrun is SMART, signing up is a statement of intent and commitment, someone else tells you what to do which reduces the stress of decision making, the group setting increases accountability, and everyone around you is genuinely thrilled for you as you progress, and when you succeed. Hence Parkrun is easy to commit to, enjoyable and provides you with a sense of achievement and community.

The great thing about working towards, and achieving something genuinely meaningful is that it is wonderfully self-motivating and self-inspiring. Confidence breeds confidence. Success builds success. After my 2 mile Road Run triumph, I immediately wanted a new target. Another seed of sporting success was being sown. The importance of consistency and taking the next step. And the next. And the next. And the next. It does not matter how small those initial steps are. If you keep inching forward, you will end up a very long way from where you started. As the saying goes, a journey of a thousand miles starts with the first step.

Again, this approach is embodied by Parkrun, and by online programmes like the one Jason Manford was doing: The next goal is always tantalisingly in reach and available to anyone: your 10, 25 or 50 runs T-shirts, a new Personal Best, a higher placing, an unbroken streak of running on consecutive weekends, promotion to 'Bronze' or 'Silver' levels and so on.

Inspired by Parkrun, I decided that my local Tri Club did not really have any beginner friendly sessions so I set up Try a Tri sessions for newcomers to the sport. I used all the strategies above and we targeted a super sprint. It was so successful that within a year, a group of Try a Tri participants did an Iron Distance triathlon as a relay. This involved a 2.4 mile swim, 112 mile bike ride and a full marathon. They called themselves The Peak Plodders and won the club's Outstanding Achievement Award that year. Not bad for people just giving tri a try!

After my first ever road run, my attention turned to the next target and I decided on the Liverpool 10K in Sefton Park. Until I had started running regularly, 10K seemed an impossible distance. That was a distance for real proper runners, not for social joggers. And yet the beauty of running (and I later found, all endurance sport) is that as long as you keep doing it, you can keep on doing more of it. The impossible suddenly looks achievable. And soon after that, it's way behind you, and you have moved onto more and more 'impossible' things. All that changes is self-belief, and the realisation that there are simply no limits. Just choices on how far you are willing to take things.

A feature of any sustained progression in any sport, however, is consistency. We cannot get better without putting in the hours regularly and consistently. Consistency needs good habits more than it needs will-power. Will-power burns out rapidly. It is far more useful to think in terms of commitment. As Bear Grylls once said, in a quote I stuck on my wall during ironman training: **Commitment is doing what you said you were going to do, long after the mood you said it in has left you.**

Deciding on a goal, writing or following a plan, entering, letting people know what you have entered, reducing mental stress as far as possible, and never questioning the decision, are features of being organised and committed. With will-power reserved for the few times when it is really challenging to commit to the plan, due to other pressures or bad weather or tiredness. Commitment means setting yourself up for success throughout the week. Will-power is just the final push to get out of the door.

You can increase your commitment by pre-committing. This means doing something upfront that makes bailing out less likely, such as agreeing to meet a friend for a ride out, booking into a lesson, signing up for an online challenge, booking the arena, asking a friend to meet you to hold your horse when you get on, or to be a foot soldier, scheduling planned sessions in your diary as if they were work meetings, and therefore not negotiable, and so on.

> **KEY CONCEPT:**
> **Commitment is far more important than will-power.**

That first 10K was a wonderful experience. Being surrounded by runners and realising I was one of them. Being cheered on by crowds. And finishing in about......68 minutes. (As I said, this is not about how I suddenly discovered a hidden talent for distance running and came in after 37 minutes. It's not that kind of story. And I'm not that kind of athlete. Truly.)

I had a few wobbly moments of feeling out of place at the start. Surrounded by skinny, sinewed greyhounds limbering up before the gun, smelling of deep heat. But another piece of the mindset puzzle is to accept that you belong. And that whatever pace you are doing is just fine.

In any sport there are a small bunch of people who want to exclude others and keep it more elite. But far more people are extremely keen to welcome newbies into their sport. Most people who love their sport want others to get into it too. You will find huge support at every level, as long as you approach it with enthusiasm and willingness.

The problem is that people self-exclude. Our own hang-ups about being too slow, or not good enough, or not having the right equipment, can lead us to reject welcoming openness, and to refuse to celebrate our own achievements.

I became acutely aware of this when I became a more established member of the running club. There was a 'fast' group, and if you had particular training goals, and did not want to wait for people, then you were free to join that. In that group you were expected to stay with the pace, or run at your own pace, and make your own way home. However, anyone who joined the 'steady' group understood that we would do turn backs, and no-one would be dropped. That was fundamental to the ethos of the club, and anyone on that run accepted and embraced it. This is the group newcomers would usually join. Inevitably, someone was always going to be last. It was often me. But sometimes someone else would come along who was slower. In which case I, or another runner, would drop back and run with them, while the whole group did turn backs from time to time. This normally worked out just fine. But some people found this intolerable and spent the entire run apologising for being so slow, berating themselves, or saying they had been wrong to come.

This is totally unhelpful, totally unnecessary, and leads to totally self-inflicted misery. I empathised because I saw myself in those runners. I felt their sense of humiliation and awkwardness, understood their need to apologise, and their wish to be anywhere else but where they were. But having moved past that type of thinking myself, I also found those runners frustrating. Not because they were slower. But because they were so down on themselves about it, which meant I was running with someone who was very evidently having a really bad time. Which – frankly – was not a lot of fun for me either. In the end there was only so much reassurance I could offer. Ultimately the person had to simply and calmly accept that, on that day, they were the slowest runner. Someone has to be – why not you? The alternative to gracious acceptance is staying miserable about it. And it really is a choice to stay miserable, though it may not feel that way.

The same pattern can often be seen in group riding lessons. Occasionally someone in a lesson struggles with, say, a particular fence. One day that person could well be you. It has certainly been me. Unless you have been placed in totally the wrong group for your ability, which can be frustrating, most people are very accepting of this. They are interested in learning how the instructor goes about persuading the horse that the jump or obstacle is manageable, because those skills are useful for any rider. They are pleased when the rider succeeds. And, to be honest, they may also be relieved that it's not them, on that particular day, who is having issues. Some riders cope perfectly well in that situation, and are happy that they are getting support for a problem. But others become angry, frustrated, upset or apologetic. Those emotional reactions are actually harder for the rest of the group to deal with than the situation itself.

This will be discussed in much more detail later when we come to talk about negative, critical and defeatist self-talk. Also known as the Parrot.

I certainly felt welcome at my first 10k and I was a long way away from last. (Not that last would have mattered. I was almost last at the Snowdon Mountain Marathon. Someone has to be.) 68 minutes was close enough to an hour for a new target to be born: going under the hour for 10K. This again was new territory: finishing events was my only goal. But having finished, well it made sense to do it again, but a bit quicker. This introduced the concept of different distances and different paces of run. Until then I only ran once a week, I ran very slowly and I ran as far as I could manage and then went home for a cup of tea. Suddenly I was entering a world of long runs and shorter runs. Pace runs and recovery runs. Recovering while out running was initially a truly bizarre concept.

The next few years were amazing in terms of my transformation from total couch potato who never ever, ever stuck to anything, to ultra-runner and ironman triathlete. 10k turned to half marathon, turned to marathon, turned to ultra-marathons, 24 hour events and multi-day stage races. Sprint tris became Olympic distance, then half ironman distance and finally a full iron distance event. That involved a 2.4 mile swim. 112 mile bike ride and a full marathon. One after the other, nonstop. Me?!

Once I began to go long, then very long, mental strength or grit became much more important, as any long distance event requires the ability to control your mind and stay positive, despite huge physical challenges. This will be discussed in more detail later in Chapters 9 and 10.

Summary

This chapter has given you multiple ideas to nudge you into being more consistent, more organized, more focused, more committed, more enthusiastic and more positive in your riding. And in any other life goal you may want to apply the same principles to.

The success of these strategies is exemplified by the extraordinary success of Parkrun, but there are many other examples of how setting SMART goals, reducing decision making stress, pre-committing to plans, seeking support and encouragement, and increasing your accountability, all add to ever greater commitment, and therefore goal achievement.

That, however, is not the whole story. Riding and other sports, particular high risk sports, have some additional challenges that can greatly interfere with your success and your enjoyment. And can sometimes paralyse you completely, so you simply feel like you can't participate in your sport at all.

CHAPTER 3

The Mental Menagerie

General mental resilience, strategies that nudge you into seeing through your plans, along with authentic motivation and a clear idea of what you do and don't want, will get you a long way in a lot of sports. But horse-riding, and other sports, raise additional challenges. We can have clear goals, along with plenty of focus and determination, but somehow still keep getting in our own way and struggling with fear, negativity, indecision and doubt. We can lose access to our skills, get stuck on plateaus or even feel like we are regressing. I explain these difficulties in terms of our 'Mental Menagerie' made up of Chimp, Parrot and Mouse.

Most problems in riding (and many in life) can be attributed to those pesky critters, living with us in our heads:

Fear lives in the limbic system; the survival centres of our brain, and I have yet to find a better description of this than the one set out in *The Chimp Paradox* by Dr Steven Peters. His metaphor of a Chimp representing our survival brain explains the issues riders have extremely well. I have adopted that metaphor in this book.

When I was working with anxious and depressed adolescents I came up with the metaphor of The Malevolent Parrot to represent those voices of criticism, negativity, doom and gloom that plague the stream of consciousness of distressed individuals. During my work with riders, the Parrot appeared repeatedly so I generalized the metaphor to include sport, changing its name to the Pesky Parrot to suggest a far more universal experience, not only endured by people with depression or anxiety, but by everyone. Or at least by most of us.

Finally, I wanted a way of talking about that voice of doubt and uncertainty. What the *Inner Game* author, Tim Gallwey, describes as Player 2, or our thinking mind. I came up with Mouse to express that idea. When Mouse shows up, we lose access to our feel and our innate abilities. We doubt our skills, so overthink and then try too hard.

Together, Chimp, Parrot and Mouse account for the vast majority of the psychological challenges and mental barriers we face as riders. They are represented by balloon animals. All 3 can be blown up out of all proportion, exerting a huge influence. But they are often full of hot air. All 3 can be popped or deflated, if you just know how. So let's get to know them.

KEY CONCEPT:
Chimp, Parrot and Mouse refer to fear, negativity and doubt. They can appear huge but can also be popped or deflated.

CHAPTER 4

Hello Chimp

That horse mad kid grew up to be a horse mad adult and I bought a pony while still at university. My pony was a friendly, sensible, willing Irish cob, who forgave me my inexperience, and looked after me. Riding was fun not sport. We mainly hacked out and often hired cross-country schooling facilities, if I could find someone to give me a lift. We did a few unaffiliated Hunter Trials for fun. I never thought of riding in terms of progression or achievement. It was just something I loved doing and never caused me stress or anxiety, let alone fear or terror.

Once I started a family, I had a lengthy break (with a few short-lived exceptions) and I did not have a horse of my own for some years, making do with the odd trekking holiday or riding lesson. Eventually my daughters started to have lessons too, and then began asking for a pony. I bought a pony for them to share, at the same time as another for me to enjoy. As my girls got more experienced they started to learn to jump. At this point a strange and unwelcome reality began to intrude.

In the years since pregnancy and motherhood, I had become scared of jumping. And I mean terrified. I realised I had rationalised my reluctance to jump, and never really explored this.

Unexamined thoughts included:

- I prefer hacking
- I'm not really into jumping anymore
- I love the countryside and going on adventures
- Jumping isn't really for me

There is nothing wrong with those thoughts – if only they were true. But in fact they were not. They were rationalisations to justify not jumping, and to stop me even asking myself why not.

> **KEY CONCEPT:**
> **Some 'choices' are actually anxiety driven rationalisations.**

During the time that I did not have a horse of my own I went to a riding centre on holiday and had a cross-country lesson. My horse slipped on the wet grass on take-off, hit the jump and somersaulted. I broke some ribs but it was not a particularly traumatic experience. I did not have flashbacks or nightmares and it was not a memory that caused me distress. I honestly never gave it much thought.

I now understand that, despite my conscious brain being fine with the accident, my survival brain had marked jumping down as a 'bad idea, best avoided'. And that 'decision' was wired into my neural circuitry. That circuitry was only fired when I was faced with the thought of jumping. Which I hadn't been for several years. The process went something like:

See a log on a hack or trail

Survival brain alerted

Assesses and says 'no thanks'

Conscious brain notes LOG = RELUCTANCE. Concludes

'I'm not really into jumping anymore'

I would avoid the log, the whole process only took about a second, and by the end of the ride was pretty much forgotten about. The survival brain advised against it, and the conscious brain obeyed, without even giving the idea serious consideration. That pattern went on for years.

However, the issue came into sharp focus when my children began to jump. I realised I could not watch them. I would literally shake. I'd feel sick. My heart would race and my palms would go sweaty. The idea of me jumping was – frankly – ridiculous. I was forced to recognise that my issue with jumping was not a conscious choice because I had found other ways to enjoy my horse, but a necessity because jumping scared the living daylights out of me.

Once I realised this, I chose to overcome it. And did. I am now jumping as confidently as I ever have in my life, with plenty of jumping dreams still ahead of me. Jumping was always the thing I loved most about riding, and still is the thing I love most about riding. But for several years that strong love of jumping was entirely hidden from my conscious mind.

Since then, I have helped many people who are terrified of different aspects of riding to understand what is going on at a brain-based level, and have helped them re-wire that part of their brain. This book will clearly explain how to go about this. No matter how terrified you are right now, you CAN ride with confidence again.

KEY CONCEPT:
Intense fear is brain-based. To overcome it, you need to re-wire your brain.

Many people will have heard of Dr Steve Peters, Psychiatrist, Performance Coach to Team SKY and the British Cycling Team, and best-selling author of *The Chimp Paradox*.

His books extends the Chimp metaphor far more than I do here, but the central idea is that the Chimp represents our biological instinct mind. We may want to jump big fences, but if the Chimp has other ideas then we have a problem.

There are many ways to ride with more confidence, fun, freedom and success. But absolutely none of those approaches are any use if you can't actually get on the horse in the first place, without having an emotional meltdown.

If this is you, then you need to understand what is happening to you. You are not being weak or pathetic, you have not bottled it, you don't hate riding, and you don't need to sell your horse and take up something safer.

It is time to get to know your Chimp. You might be very irritated with him and he may be making your life extremely difficult, but the Chimp is your biological brain. His mission in life is to keep you safe. So, really, he's trying to help.

KEY CONCEPT:
The Chimp's priority is safety. He will act to protect himself if he believes he is in danger.

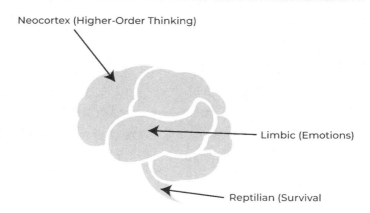

Neocortex (Higher-Order Thinking)

Limbic (Emotions)

Reptilian (Survival

We have 3 brains. The reptilian brain is the oldest, controlling things like heart rate and temperature. We don't need to worry about that.

The limbic system is our mammalian brain. This is where emotion sits. Dr Peters described those parts of the brain as The Chimp.

The human brain is our logical, reasoning brain, located in the neo-cortex – literally 'new brain'. These are the functions that have evolved most recently. Sophisticated, higher order thinking is unique to humans. But these clever, thinking processes are overlaid onto fully functional animal-instincts, which still exert huge influence on us all.

The Chimp operates on instinct. He acts first and asks questions later. Actually he does not ask questions at all. Rather he acts, and leaves YOU – the human – asking the questions. Like 'why did I look down into the ditch AGAIN', 'Why did I take my leg off on the approach to the jump AGAIN' and 'why does that 30cm fence look like it's a mountain?'

The Chimp wants a few different things in life, including status and success. So, once tamed, the Chimp can be a fantastic ally in your quest to up your game. But his overriding priority is survival. He wants to keep himself and you alive. But he evolved a very long time ago and has no idea about what is truly dangerous in the modern world. Poor Chimp – he is a fish out of water. Well actually, he's a Chimp no longer in the jungle, but does not know it.

When it comes to survival, the Chimp operates according to a very simple system:

Anxiety = danger.
No anxiety = safe.

Whatever you do that creates anxiety, he will assume to be dangerous. Whatever you do that reduces the anxiety, he assumes made the danger go away.

Read that again as this is absolutely crucial to your understanding.

KEY CONCEPT:

In Chimp-World the thing you did to reduce the anxiety is the thing that took away the danger.

Let's take a brief detour to the world of Obsessive Compulsive Disorder (OCD).

In OCD, a thought or idea generates anxiety. Such as 'the plane my sister is on right now will crash unless I say this magical phrase over and over again.'

The anxiety gives credibility to this idea, and the person feels compelled to repeat random phrases to prevent something terrible from happening. The anxiety reduces and Chimp goes AHA! Repeating that phrase kept that plane in the air.

The person with OCD recognizes, at the human level, that this is absurd, but at the Chimp-Brain level it makes perfect sense. Whatever the person did that took away the anxiety, is the thing that took away the danger.

Therefore, telling a person with OCD not to repeat the phrase, makes that person feel that they would be putting everyone on the plane at serious risk.

What does that mean for your riding?

Well let's say that the thought of getting on a horse makes you feel anxious. But you are brave and you get on anyway. Your Chimp goes into overdrive: GET OFF, GET OFF, WE ARE GOING TO DIE!!

Anxiety spikes to a level you find intolerable and so you get off. Anxiety drops. Chimp concludes: Getting off SAVED OUR LIFE. Phew, thank heavens we got off just in time.

Once the Chimp has decided (via anxiety) that riding is dangerous, no amount of reasoning, courage or will-power will change his mind. He has to learn through experience that riding is not imminently life threatening, every time you sit on a horse.

The bad news is you have to go through some anxiety during the re-training process. The good news is the Chimp learns really fast. After all, in the jungle he needs to run from snakes, but would tire and die rapidly if he ran from everything long and bendy. Like vines. He needs to be adaptable, and to rapidly change his mind based on his experiences about what is and is not dangerous. The best news is this is really, really easy to do. Honestly. I'd love to claim to have some sort of magic touch to be able to get a person from complete meltdown to happily trotting round in a few minutes, but actually it is easy. However, it is counter-intuitive and also very, very easy to get wrong. In other words, this is a problem that can be fixed in minutes but can also persist for years.

> **KEY CONCEPT:**
> **The Chimp can't be reasoned with. He needs to learn from experience.**

Re-wiring the Chimp Brain

The biological brain only learns through experience. We can't reason with the Chimp. We have to demonstrate that the Chimp is over-estimating danger. And we do that using the only language he understands: by manipulating ANXIETY.

The extreme anxiety triggered when you think about riding or try to ride is essentially a 'Fight or Flight' reaction triggered when you are not in extreme danger. Think of it as a faulty smoke alarm going off in your head when there is no fire.

The Circle of Stress!

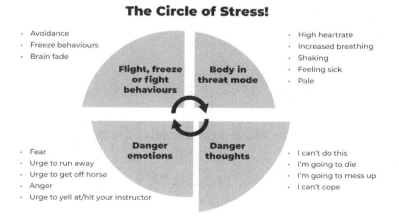

- Avoidance
- Freeze behaviours
- Brain fade

Flight, freeze or fight behaviours

Body in threat mode

- High heartrate
- Increased breathing
- Shaking
- Feeling sick
- Pale

- Fear
- Urge to run away
- Urge to get off horse
- Anger
- Urge to yell at/hit your instructor

Danger emotions

Danger thoughts

- I can't do this
- I'm going to die
- I'm going to mess up
- I can't cope

Flight, Freeze or Fight are the Chimp's survival mechanisms.

Any time your Chimp feels under threat, he responds instinctively and the body goes into 'Threat Mode'.

These changes equip the body to fend off the danger by playing dead via freezing, running away faster or fighting more ferociously.

Once these bodily changes occur, a vicious circle begins: we notice these changes and start having Danger Thoughts. A combination of a body in threat mode, plus danger thoughts, amplifies the anxiety/fear. This emotion leads to strong behavioural urges to run away (flight), to freeze or to fight. By running away, or avoiding, we fail to teach the Chimp that our perceptions of the risks are distorted, so his belief that riding is dangerous is maintained or increased.

To tame our Chimp we need to deal with all of these quadrants separately:

i)   We need to deal with the physiological changes, and calm our bodies

ii) We need to soothe the Chimp by addressing danger thoughts, and thinking more rationally and positively

iii) We need to reduce the sense of threat to reduce fear

iv) We need to stop obeying the Chimp when we have the urge to flee or freeze.

The first 3 approaches all serve the purpose of calming the Chimp down just enough so that you can follow through with quadrant iv. Changing your behaviour, and therefore changing the Chimp's experiences of riding, is the only thing that actually re-wires the brain.

The following chapter will go through each section in turn. But let's first explore, in a little more detail, how the Chimp operates, and why you feel the way you do.

Let's meet Cherry. Cherry wants to ride but the very thought of riding makes her panic. At our first session she described the feelings in her body, the thoughts running through her mind, the emotions she is feeling and the urges she is having.

Feelings:
I feel sick, shaky and I want to cry.

Thoughts:
I can't do it. I'm going to die. She might buck me off or run off. I can't get on. There's no way.

Emotions:
I am petrified

Behavioural Urges:
Run a mile. Not go near the horse.

Cherry did try to ride every so often. She was reassured that she would be fine. Her instructor had her on a lead rope. She used courage and determination to get on. But once she was on the horse, her fear rose even higher, and she began to sob. She managed about 10 minutes, on the lead rein, clinging on to a neck strap, then got off at the point of highest anxiety. Her fear of riding was not reduced by having managed to ride. In fact, she was more anxious than ever because it had been such an awful experience, and because she just confirmed to the Chimp that riding was dangerous, and the only way back to safety was getting off.

The mistake Cherry made was trying to manage the Chimp with reassurance and logic, when the Chimp's only language is emotion.

Logically knowing she was safe was enough to get her on the horse, but it was not remotely effective at soothing a distraught Chimp.

Another example comes from my own experiences when I started competing. Picture the scene: stroppy, stressed rider is telling her long-suffering friend, 'why did I ever agree to this, I hate competing, I'd rather be anywhere else but here! I am never, ever, ever doing this ever again.'

That was me in the cross-country warm-up during a long hold on the course, just before I was due to go down to the start box. My first event on my horse, Amber, and my first BE event, ever.

Had you been a fly on the wall at that event, you may also have seen my great friend trying to encourage me, and me riding away from her, muttering swear words under my breath. (Sorry, Cris). That is Flight and

Fight in action. The following is my blog post reflecting on that competition.

Amber The Event Horse:

Well it's official. I wasn't eliminated, I have a score (albeit rather a bad one!!) therefore I have successfully negotiated a BE Event with my awesome orange pony-partner. I am, she is, we are EVENTERS. Woop woop. I am so happy with her I could cry. In fact I have. Alongside the silly grin that keeps breaking out over my face.

Her dressage was as good as I could expect it to be really.

She did nothing wrong and the judge described her as a 'smart horse' which I assume refers to her innate qualities and not my imperfect turn out skills – she only has half a mane after a winter of full necked rugs and she wasn't plaited. And she bathed in mud all day yesterday. So anyway, SHE did nothing wrong. Her ditzy driver however did go wrong. TWICE. Quite impressive, especially as the only course error I made was getting to the final centre line. (Yes wrong at the same place. Yes twice).

Then show-jumping – she was forward and keen but not totally out of control which is always nice. She had 4 faults. Her ditzy driver however went wrong. Argggghhhhh. I was setting her up nicely for number 8 as I went merrily past number 7 and had to circle back. Oh dear. Still we were never going to trouble the leader-board anyway and so I was far more interested in how she went than where we came. And she was great.

That meant the dreaded cross-country was up next. And I was absolutely terrified after walking the course. Jumps seem a lot bigger when you aren't looking down at them from a 16.3 powerhouse of a horse! I felt sicker and sicker as I went past number 3 (huge table), number 5 (weird pink thing), number 7 (big hanging log downhill), numbers 9 & 10 (skinny related distances), number 14 (ski jump), number 19 (huge brush with a drop the other side). Oh help. I just could not see how Amber would jump them all.

She was very excited during the warm-up, which added to my apprehension. Nerves were not improved by a 40 minute delay on the course when a rider came off. Then another 10 minute course delay a few horses later. Sobering reminders of the stakes we are playing with in this game. By the time I was walking over to the start box I had pretty much decided I was never, ever putting myself through this again. My aim to not be eliminated had morphed into a simple wish to come home safe.

And then my awesome horse just took off and flew everything as if she has been doing this all her life. Not one moment of hesitation or doubt. It was very clear pretty quickly that she was going to jump whatever she was presented to. All I had to do was get her in front of each fence vaguely straight. Not that that was entirely straightforward! She was very, VERY keen.

First ODE and no cross-country jumping faults! I am humbled and amazed by this horse. And I can't wait for our next run. So it looks like I will be putting myself through it again after all.

All the Chimp behaviours were present: total terror at the thought of jumping and reluctance to ever do it again (flight), brain fog, which caused TWO errors of course in dressage (freeze). Yet more brain fog, which led to a missed fence in show-jumping, (freeze again). Fight showed up in my warm-up tantrum where I muttered and swore under my breath at my lovely, long-suffering friend. Then adrenaline kicked in for cross-country and Chimp suddenly felt invincible. This is FIGHT, of the 'fire in your belly' type. Which is far more useful than the 'shout at your poor friend' type.

The human – me – loved it and could not wait to go again. The joy, the thrill, the love of eventing is REAL. That is me, driven by intrinsic motivation. Best way to spend a day. Ever. The rest was Chimp, and I needed to find a way to tame him so that I could cope better with the build-up, and ride better once we got going.

Summary

The Chimp is our biological instinct brain and exerts a powerful influence over you, whenever he perceives a situation to be threatening. We cannot ignore our Chimp, nor override him. Equally we should not confuse his ideas and preferences for our own true wishes. We need to tame him, and eventually persuade him that he wants what we want. Chapter 5 explains how.

Chimp Taming Strategies

Managing FIGHT or FLIGHT Reactions

Have another look at that diagram.

The Circle of Stress!

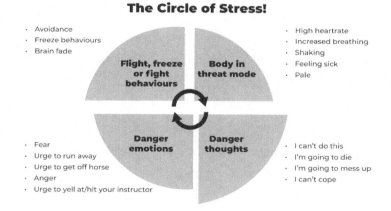

- Avoidance
- Freeze behaviours
- Brain fade

Flight, freeze or fight behaviours

Body in threat mode

- High heartrate
- Increased breathing
- Shaking
- Feeling sick
- Pale

- Fear
- Urge to run away
- Urge to get off horse
- Anger
- Urge to yell at/hit your instructor

Danger emotions

Danger thoughts

- I can't do this
- I'm going to die
- I'm going to mess up
- I can't cope

Chimp Taming requires us to address every quadrant:

i) Calming your Body: We need to deal with the physiological changes
ii) Calming your Mind: We need to soothe the Chimp by addressing danger thoughts and thinking more rationally and positively

iii) Calming our emotions: We need to reducing our sense of danger, to reduce fear

iv) Changing our behaviour: We need to stop obeying the Chimp when we have the urge to flee, freeze or fight

i-iii are helpful in taking the edge off your fear just enough so we can achieve iv, which is the step that actually re-wires the Chimp brain.

Calming Your Body

There is a strong mind-body link. What your body is doing sends signals to the brain, which responds by releasing hormones that affect how the body feels. When we are in fight and flight mode, our sympathetic nervous system is active. This is the stress response system designed to help us in situations of danger. A perception of threat leads to the release of stress hormones, adrenaline and cortisol, which then affect the body, and make us feel agitated and tense.

However, we also have the parasympathetic nervous system: the rest and digest system. When the parasympathetic nervous system is active, the Chimp feels calmer. We can actively seek to dampen down the fight and flight sympathetic nervous system response in several ways.

Breathing

Breathing correctly is crucial for relaxation and focus. There are many interventions based purely on breathing, from Wim Hof's deep breathing method to Breathworks, an international mindfulness organization based around mindfulness of breathing.

Your breathing matters hugely to both you and to your horse. Horses hold their breath when they sense danger so they can hear more clearly, and if one herd member does this, the whole herd is alerted. If you are holding your breath, your horse will know, and may well become tense, assuming you have noticed something you are worried about.

There are dozens of methods to help you breathe more effectively. You can experiment with what works for you, but the key elements are simple:

1) Your diaphragm must sink so you are belly breathing, and not just breathing into your upper chest.

2) You need to reverse the tendency when anxious to breathe in more than you breathe out (panting, or hyperventilating), to breathe fast and irregularly, or to hold your breath.

Diaphragmatic or Belly Breathing

Place your hands across your belly with fingertips just touching. As you breathe in, the fingertips should move apart. As you breathe out, they should come back together again. This means you are dropping your diaphragm and your belly is expanding. Practice this at home till it becomes second nature to breathe this way.

Paced Breathing & Box Breathing

Paced breathing is a slow, deliberate deep breathing exercise, sustained for a specific period of time. Paced breathing has been researched widely, to examine its effectiveness, and it has been found to be beneficial for a variety of issues, both physical and psychological.

It is useful to slow your breathing by counting breaths, with a longer out-breath than in-breath. For example, breathe in to the count of 5 and breathe out to the count of 7. I do this whenever I first get on my horse, linking the counting to the horse's footfalls. If you are anxious you may need to start with a 3,5 ratio until you begin to relax, and your breathing naturally slows. Then you can move to 4,6 or 7,9, or whatever feels comfortable.

Box breathing is probably the most well-known process, recommended by Dr Jenny Susser, a Clinical Sport Psychologist, specialising in horse riding. This has a 4-4-4-4 ratio: breathe in for the count of 4, hold for 4, breathe out for 4, and hold for 4, then repeat, while visualizing breathing round the 4 sides of a box. I have personally found that Box breathing encourages me to hold my breath, and I forget where I am on the box, but I'd encourage you to try different exercises, and discover what works for you.

There are lots of apps out there that can help guide you through paced breathing, and these have a strong evidence base.

Mindfulness of Breathing

This is an off-horse exercise and differs from paced breathing in that you simply observe your breath, rather than deliberately seeking to slow your breathing down, and make it more regular. A popular practice is to think of breath as circular. Notice breath coming in, turning round, going out; coming in, turning round, going out. You will begin to notice the subtle changes through the entire cycle. It is common to add in visualisations, like breathing in white light and breathing out dark smoke, representing negativity or tension, or to imagine breathing from different body parts such as your hands or the top of your head. Mindfulness of breathing is a tradition going back thousands of years, with extremely well documented health benefits. I would strongly recommend you use an app or CD, or attend classes, to establish the practice correctly.

We can also use other parts of our body to communicate with our brain, and interrupt the stress response.

Half-Smile

We use over 20 muscles in the face when we smile, and if you use a half-smile these muscles will be activated. They then send signals to the brain which helps the brain feel more relaxed, and more accepting of whatever is happening. Start by letting go of tension and relaxing your face, jaw, neck, shoulders, and half-smile with your lips. A half-smile is slightly upturned lips with a relaxed face and a serene facial expression. A full, false smile might tell your brain you are hiding or faking the emotion, and a grimace communicates the opposite of what you want, so ensure you are not grinning manically. Instead, just move the corners of your mouth upward ever so slightly, while softening and relaxing the jaw.

Confident Posture

When we are anxious we try to make ourselves small, to be invisible or inoffensive to potential predators. An extreme version of a defensive, anxious posture is the foetal position. The opposite of this is the power pose, in which you take up space, legs slightly apart, chest out, head held high, making eye contact. Research has shown that privately power posing for 2 minutes before a job interview makes candidates feel more confident. They are also perceived as more confident by interviewers. You can power pose before you get on a horse, communicating to your brain that you feel positive and confident. Once you are on the horse you can also send these same positivity messages to your brain by sitting up straight, taking up space, chest wide in an open posture, head up and looking ahead, not down. The phrase 'chin up' exists for a reason. Lift your chin and you automatically feel better. This is an active, athletic posture, and therefore good for riding anyway, and transmits the message to your brain, and your horse, that you feel ready for anything up there.

KEY CONCEPT:
Brain-body links mean that calming your body reduces your anxiety

Calming Your Mind

Mental Processing

When the Chimp is worried, he diverts blood from the thinking brain to the emotion brain and to the major muscle groups needed for running and fighting. So when people say they can't think straight when they come down the centre line in a dressage test, well that's why. The thinking brain is deprived of blood, and not functioning properly.

You can force blood back up to this part of your brain by making yourself consciously think about neutral topics. Ask yourself questions like 'what did I have for breakfast this morning' or 'what colour socks do I have on.' Use your brain by doing mental arithmetic, such as counting down from 100 in 7s: 100, 93, 86 etc. Don't let thinking drift into auto-pilot. It does not matter much what you think about, as long as it does not involve any frightening or negative thoughts, and you are actively using mental processing, forcing blood to return to the rational, reasoning brain.

Visualisations

Visualisations result in 2 powerful effects: reducing anxiety and increasing skill.

Movement is initiated in the brain, so when you vividly imagine doing something, the relevant areas of the brain light up. When you imagine getting on, the horse bucking, and you falling off, the areas of your brain involved in clinging on, being thrown off, and fear are activated. Not surprisingly, this generates more fear, and increased reluctance to ever get on, even though nothing has actually happened. But the reverse is equally powerful: if you imagine getting on and going for a nice stroll around the arena, with nothing bad happening, the areas of the brain involved in sitting in the saddle in walk, and feeling relaxed become activated. This then reduces anxiety and reluctance to get on.

When I first decided I wanted to start jumping again I could not even look at a jump. So step 1 for me involved just looking at fences. Then imagining jumping them until I could visualize going over a small cross-pole without sweating, shaking or feeling sick. Only then was actually jumping a realistic possibility.

The effectiveness of visualisations is supported by psychological therapies. 'Imaginal exposure' (the technical term for visualisation) is a standard part of cognitive-behavioural therapy for all types of anxiety disorders, including phobias, generalized anxiety disorder, OCD and PTSD.

I can't emphasise enough how valuable visualisations are at helping you reduce anxiety, access your skills, and ride to your ability. And even, astonishingly, they can *improve* your riding skills, without even needing to get on your horse.

Top athletes in every sport visualise important elements of their practice. Whether it is serving at matchpoint, jumping a tricky line, sinking a 30 foot putt or executing a perfect dive.

Tiger Woods has been using it since he was a young child. Jack Niklaus has stated he never hits a shot without having visualised it first. Athletes use vivid, highly detailed visualisations, engaging all their senses, within this form of mental rehearsal.

Visualisations do far more than just reduce anxiety. As movement is initiated in the brain, you strengthen neural pathways for movements, just by imagining them. This creates genuine practice effects, all from the comfort of your sofa.

A study looking at brain patterns in weightlifters found that the patterns activated when a weightlifter lifted hundreds of pounds were similarly activated when they only imagined lifting. A study comparing finger strength as a result of working out, versus imagined work-outs, found that the work-out group improved strength by 58% over the course of the programme. But those who just imagined working out also improved by 35%.

Crucially, you practice *well* in imagination. You can ride flawlessly, choosing your line perfectly, looking ahead, maintaining good form, accessing all your skills, and staying in perfect balance, on a 100% reliable horse who never tires.

Visualisations can improve motor control, attention, perception, planning, and memory. People are far more likely to ride good lines or test movements, to think and plan ahead, to choose the correct canter or tempo, and to maintain form and balance, if they have mentally rehearsed the round or test first.

Your brain is literally being trained for enhanced performance during visualisation. So it is no surprise that it has been found that regularly practicing in this way can enhance motivation, confidence and self-efficacy, and increase the likelihood that you ride in that magical state of 'flow', at the peak of your ability, where everything feels effortless and easy.

KEY CONCEPT:
Visualisations reduce anxiety, increase confidence, and even increase skill

Calming Our Emotions, Reducing Fear

There are 3 components to fear. When all 3 are present, we feel scared.

1) A sense of danger
2) A sense of incompetence
3) A sense of vulnerability

Lack of competence would not be experienced as frightening if you were on very safe horse, or on a lead rein. Awareness of danger would not feel frightening if you felt competent to navigate the challenge. Neither incompetence nor danger seem to frighten people who feel invulnerable. This applies to quite a few young kids and some kamikaze adults. But it's not recommended! However, we experience fear when an awareness of danger, a lack of confidence in our ability to cope, and a sense of our own vulnerability, are all present.

Fear both magnifies, and is magnified by, these 3 elements.

Fear heightens your sense of danger. Jumps look enormous. Banks look like sheer precipices. A forward canter feels like a flat-out gallop. These distorted perceptions make us more scared, and those fears amplify the distorted perceptions. This triggers doubt in our ability to manage, so our sense of competency reduces. Once in that anxious and doubting headspace, our fear and sense of danger are further magnified. We end up believing we are facing an impossible challenge, that we are entirely unable to cope with, and that makes us feel extremely vulnerable.

I recognized this pattern in my fear of jumping. Jumps just looked HUGE. I don't mean that I knew they were small but felt they were still too big for me. I mean I literally saw them as enormous.

The Chimp scans for, and exaggerates, any risks he identifies, as this is crucial for survival. We need our attention to be alerted, and then we need to SEE the threat. If you are scared of spiders, and see one out of the corner of your eye, it will usually look far bigger than it really is.

When I was just beginning to learn to jump again I set myself the challenge of doing a series of three logs on the farm ride around the yard I was on. Two looked pretty small, even to me, but the third looked massive. I called it 'the big log'. It felt like a lifetime's ambition to jump it. I honestly felt that if I could jump that I'd never want to go higher. That was the pinnacle of my ambition. The day I finally did it, I felt like we had jumped the moon. I was ecstatic.

A few years later I had left that yard, but was walking my dog on the farm ride with my daughter. I saw a tiny log where the big log used to be.

'I wonder why they got rid of the big log', I remarked.

'Mum, that is the big log' she replied. I could not reconcile the huge trunk in my mind's eye with this 40cm branch in front of me. But it was the same jump.

In a similar vein, I was having a jumping lesson a few months after starting to jump again. A straight rail was put up with a filler underneath. I asked, in all seriousness, 'how do you know my horse can jump that?'

'A Shetland pony could jump that!' came the reply. It was probably about 50cm high. It looked enormous.

We can address fear by dealing with all 3 of the factors that lead us to feel afraid: reducing the sense of danger, increasing our sense of competence, and addressing our sense of vulnerability.

Addressing Distorted Perceptions

It is helpful to properly look at fences, to shrink them in your mind's eye. Alternatively, do the precise opposite, and simply refuse to look at them at all, knowing that they will look bigger than they really are. Look over them, not at them, and ride them exactly the same way as you do smaller jumps. Experiment and see what works for you. I regularly do both: If I can walk around a cross-country schooling field before a lesson or in a warm-up, then I do the fence shrinking exercise below. If the jumps go up in a show-jumping lesson, and start looking 'too high', I simply trust my instructor, and look up and over, rather than at the fence.

Fence Shrinking Exercise

Ride around a cross-country schooling field in walk and approach bigger fences than you plan to jump, as if you are jumping them. Visualise coming in canter, landing in balance, and riding away. Even though you know you are not going to jump them, simply imagining it often makes palms go a bit sweaty and heart rate to rise. Which is why it works. You are facing the fear without actually doing anything remotely risky. Look at each jump carefully: where would you ride that line? What is the ground line like?

I do this often and, in this way, the 100cm or novice fences stop looking like 5* ones and become fences that – while too big for my current level of training – are clearly jumpable. Then when the lesson starts, the 90cm fences I am actually jumping have shrunk back to a sensible size.

Embrace Speed

Our perception of speed can also be distorted. We can feel as if we are going far faster than we are, and that the horse is out of control when, really, he is just travelling nicely. Obviously, horses can be out of control, which is unsafe, but often they are fine, just fast. We can become more aware of speed, and more comfortable with it, by moving through the gears. We can assign canter 3 speeds: 1,2,3. A steady canter, a travelling canter and a forward canter. Move up and down, paying attention to the subtle changes, and experimenting with how easy it feels to adjust. In this way you can begin to trust that speed is not scary if you are in control. Whereas a horse can 'run off' with you in walk. Speed and control are not the same thing. You can be in control at higher speeds and out of control at lower ones.

KEY CONCEPT:
The Chimp magnifies the sense of threat which makes us feel more scared.

Another element that contributes to fear, alongside a sense of danger and vulnerability, is the belief that we are not up to the challenge. That we are not competent enough to do what we are trying to do. Nor are we capable of dealing with anything that might go wrong.

Increasing your Sense of Competence: Connect to your Skills

How do you sum up your riding identity?

Grab a piece of paper and write down whatever words come to mind when you consider your riding.

It might look something like this:

- Unbalanced
- Nervous
- Not making much progress
- Stuck
- Unstable lower leg
- Frustrated
- Confused
- Struggling with independent seat.
- Would not cope if things went wrong
- Scared to get on

That is your personal riding 'culture'. Is it a winning formula?

At my confidence camps I sometimes ask people to write down 20 positive things about their riding. Most people find it difficult to come up with any. If I switch the task, and ask people to identify 20 things they are struggling with, the lists fill up immediately.

If we have any issues, whatsoever, at any time, they all 'count' as a negative and go on the list. If we have any positives, at any time, unconfident riders tend to examine them from all angles. For example you may think:

'I am in balance over fences. Does that one count? No there was that time I lost balance over that jump 3 weeks ago.'

'Soft hands? No there was that time I jabbed her in the mouth.'

'Quiet hands? No that video from my lesson was awful.'

'Good lower leg – oh but it sometimes swings back. And it's not that stable in canter transitions.'

'Independent seat? Good god, no!'

Even if we think of something we can definitely do – 'I've nailed rising trot' – we discount that as an achievement: 'Oh great I can finally trot after 25 years of riding. Marvellous.'

And yet we do not apply this rigid exclusion criteria to our 'faults'.

'Unbalanced in 1 jump in 20.' Yep, unbalanced over fences at times can go down.

'Hands far stiller than they used to be but still don't look like Lottie Fry.' Let's put down unsteady hands. And so on.

When it comes to acknowledging our skills, riders are particularly self-critical. I have often wondered if the problem is that, for some entirely illogical reason, we expect to be able to ride like the best riders in the world.

Maybe it's because the skill involved in riding like the best riders in the world is not immediately obvious.

Picture an Olympic gymnast doing a floor routine. All that twisting and tumbling. Gravity defying and mesmerising. How? Just *how*? Now picture the dressage test at Badminton. Can you do that? Well yes, mostly. We may not do it *well*, but there is nothing the riders at Badminton are doing in a test that we could not have a go at. And yet those riders are as good at riding as those gymnasts are good at gymnastics. Why do we expect to look and ride like them?

We need to stop fault-finding, and start celebrating improvements. We need to stop expecting to be perfect, and be happy with a bit better than before. And we need to stop dismissing the many, many riding skills we have, and instead become better knowing what we are good at.

By all means, be aware of the aspects that need more work, the areas of relative weakness. Progress requires working on those limiters. But we can go so far down the road of self-criticism that we can almost feel as though we can hardly ride at all, even when we are actually highly competent in lots of ways.

As an exercise, I'd like you to connect to your skills. Write down all the things you are good at. And do not allow yourself to discount or ignore qualities. Keep going till you have reached 20. And in the spirit of self-disclosure, I did this too. It went something like:

I can walk and trot in balance

I can mostly canter in balance (putting this in though I am telling myself I lose balance in transitions)

Balance in transitions improving. (Ha! Caught the parrot attempt to discount)

Hands getting quieter (Parrot shouting; A TINY BIT QUIETER AND THEY ARE STILL AWFUL)

Position over jumps more secure (Parrot drawing my attention to the odd loss of balance that can still happen)

Increasing awareness of what my horse is doing under me

Increasing awareness of canter quality: feeling what I am after

Better at looking ahead.

I work hard

I try to be fair to the horse

I rarely fall off

I can sit a spook or a buck.

Etc

This often feels excruciating to do at first. But it is very helpful for enhancing your feelings of competence, and should be regularly repeated as you gain more skills.

KEY CONCEPT:
Being aware of your competencies can reduce your sense of fear.

Reducing our Sense of Vulnerability: Stop "What-Iffing."

We also increase our trust in our competence, and reduce our feelings of vulnerability, by developing a more realistic sense of what might happen when we ride. Unless we are totally over-horsed, our horses are likely to be suitably matched to us. If they aren't, that is a different problem, so let's assume you are on a horse who you have the skills to ride, and that you are generally capable of dealing effectively and safely with whatever challenging behaviours he presents.

Of course, horses are living, breathing animals and can behave in unexpected ways. But if we allow fear of the unexpected to dominate our thinking, then we will no longer be riding the real, mostly trustworthy horse we are actually on, and are instead riding an imaginary, unpredictable, snorting dragon of a beast. Exaggerating the risks of the horse doing something we would not be able to cope with makes us feel vulnerable.

There are additional disadvantages to this. Firstly, if we are anticipating a problem, and feel vulnerable and anxious, we are more likely to create a real problem. I once helped out at a riding centre and a debate raged among ride leaders about whether or not to warn riders about a 'scary stone'. This was a huge boulder resting on the side of the trail, half way along a canter track. One group of ride leaders said that horses can shy at it, so riders need to be prepared for that. The other group said that if riders expected the horses to shy, more would. They all recognised that in a ride of around 10 horses, about 5 would shy in the pre-warned group. Only 1-2 (if any) would shy in the non-warned group. However, a rider was more likely to come off. So it was a dilemma, but the take-home message is that if you are worrying about your horse shying at the 'scary stone', (or in the spooky corner, or because of the wind, or, or....) then he is far more likely to do so.

If we ride anticipating danger, we communicate danger to the horse, who switches onto higher alert. In that way, we create the problems we are fearing.

Another disadvantage is that if you are worrying about that hedge over there, you are not HERE. You lose feel for what is actually going on underneath you, because you have become focused on potential hazards in the distance. That disconnect means you are far less likely to feel an issue before it turns into any sort of significant reaction.

Buck Brannaman once said 'It's about what happens before what happens, happens.' If you are horizon scanning for danger, then you won't notice any build-up in the here and now. Being tuned into your horse and fully present, rather than focused on an imaginary and feared future, makes you much more able to avert an issue before anything has happened.

Staying rooted in reality also means you are more able to deal with any challenging situations that do arise.

I vividly recall a hack shortly after getting my new horse, Amber, where this skill was put to the test. Amber features a lot in this book, and can be best described as a Ferrari being ridden by a person better suited to a Ford. A good friend had a safe, steady horse and she agreed to ride out with me the first time I took Amber into the big wide world. We were planning on a nice relaxed amble down a valley: slow, steady and ideally entirely drama-free. However, as we entered the valley system and turned a corner, we saw a herd of young cows. They were immediately curious about us, and gathered en masse to follow behind. Closely behind. Then a brave herd leader started running up to us, dropping back, then running at us again. Visions of a mass stampede and crazy rodeo scenes flooded my brain. I was on a horse I barely knew. Had she ever seen cows? Was she the spinning, bolting type? What was she going to do? And what were the damn cows going to do?! My brain froze as my attention was transfixed on what I feared was *about* to happen. Not on what was actually happening.

Luckily my friend was on a horse she had built a great partnership with. And, handily, had taken to cowboy camp. I also managed to get my brain back into the here and now, and off the 'what if' scenarios I was scared of.

My job was to stay totally calm and relaxed on Amber, to communicate 'all is well'. Which I did by singing

Glen Campbell's Rhinestone Cowboy over and over again, to help me breathe, and make myself laugh. My friend's job was to turn and face the cows, to push them back whenever they got too close. We stayed relaxed, walking slowly, and dealing with the situation effectively, until we got to a gate and could shut it behind us, leaving them behind. Staying present and dealing with the situation calmly, was much more effective than freezing and freaking would have been.

In addition, if you are riding while focused on the imaginary dangers in your mind, then you will ride to avoid what you don't want rather than riding to create what you do want. It is far more effective to picture and feel what you are after, and to ride for that. If the horse deviates from that, don't follow the horse to where he has gone – just keep what you want in mind, and continue focusing on that. In this way riding stops being a series of over-corrections, but instead becomes a seamless process of continuous communication about what you are asking for from the horse.

Finally, riding the horse you actually have underneath you, instead of the imaginary horse you fear, means you allow the horse to be different day-to-day. You don't have a pre-conceived idea of how the horse will be or go. We therefore allow the horse to be as we find them in that moment, and we are more sensitive and attuned to how they are feeling, and how they are going. This makes us better riders.

KEY CONCEPT:
Ride the horse actually underneath you, not the imaginary one in your mind. This both increases your competence, and reduces your sense of vulnerability.

Changing Behaviour

This is the most crucial part of Chimp taming as this is the thing that will actually re-wire the Chimp brain. The strategies to calm the body, minimise the danger thoughts, and reduce the fear are important because they help you calm the Chimp down enough, so that you can change your behaviour. Without behaviour change, you will not overcome your fear or gain confidence. You need to address the Flight and Freeze behaviours.

Dealing with Flight

The Chimp only learns through experience. In particular, the Chimp will learn that whatever you were doing when the anxiety dropped is safe.

Let's reconsider the experience of Cherry. Her anxiety dropped when she got off the horse, and the Chimp concluded that getting off saved her from harm, and that staying on would have been dangerous. The Chimp's belief that riding is dangerous was not, in any way, reduced by her experience. Instead, it was re-confirmed.

But what would have happened if Cherry had managed to stay on? Remember she was perfectly safe, as she was on a steady horse in halt on a lead rein. At some point, anxiety would have plateaued as it can only go so high. And it can't stay at that height for very long. Within a few minutes the anxiety would have begun to drop, while Cherry was still on the horse. This process is called habituation.

Allowing anxiety to habituate, while still doing the feared activity, is fundamental to re-wiring the brain and re-educating the Chimp.

KEY CONCEPT:
Habituation is the process by which anxiety drops, while you are still doing the feared activity. Habituation is essential for overcoming strong fear reactions.

Exposure to the Feared Situation

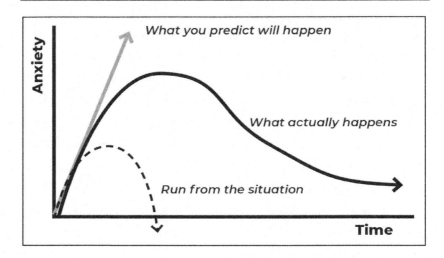

The above diagram shows a typical response when you do something that scares you, and triggers a strong fear reaction.

The anxiety rises rapidly. The person tends to believe that the anxiety will just carry on getting worse and worse forever (the straight line). They therefore often escape the situation while anxiety is still high or rising, (the short curved line). Anxiety drops rapidly and the Chimp concludes that you were genuinely in danger, and that running away is the thing that made you safer. Remember, in Chimp-World: anxiety = danger. Reduced anxiety = safety.

However if the person stays in the situation, the anxiety peaks, and then drops, as shown by the longer line.

It is this drop, while doing the feared activity, that re-educates the Chimp, in the process of habituation.

The Chimp will conclude that whatever you were doing at the point the anxiety dropped is the thing that reduced the danger. In the case of the short curved line, getting off the horse (running from the situation) is what the Chimp believed made the danger go away. So the Chimp will inevitably want to reduce the danger exactly the same way next time, convinced that riding is dangerous and the only way to reduce that danger is to get off.

However, when Cherry stayed on the horse, the anxiety dropped while she was still mounted. This was a totally new experience for the Chimp, who therefore had to re-evaluate what is and is not dangerous.

Repeated Exposure

Unfortunately, you can't just do this once. The Chimp needs to re-learn over time, and the secret of success is to repeat the exercise over and over again. However, each time, the anxiety goes a little less high, and reduces a little more quickly.

It may be quicker and easier to book a session with someone who understands how habituation works. But it is also possible to sort this by yourself, through a process called graded exposure.

Setting up a Graded Exposure Programme

Rate your anxiety on a scale of 1-10, with 1 being no anxiety at all, and 10 being totally overwhelmed with anxiety.

Mentally run through a feared situation and try to work out the point at which anxiety rises, but does not go so high that you are too overwhelmed to continue. Maybe that is standing at a mounting block. Maybe it's walking around an arena on a lead rein. Maybe it is riding in open spaces or jumping a small cross-pole.

In Cherry's case, this was standing next to the mounting block, with the horse prepared for mounting.

Do the activity that scares you, and rate your anxiety on a scale of 1-10.

You will probably find the anxiety goes up, then stays the same, then begins to drop. *Stay with the activity* until the anxiety has dropped.

It is the anxiety dropping, while you are still doing the thing that scares you, that re-wires the Chimp brain and helps the Chimp re-evaluate what is and is not dangerous.

Once anxiety is down at 5 or lower, or has dropped at least 3 points, stop the task and have a short break. Then repeat.

The key is *repeated, prolonged exposure.*

A typical pattern looks like this: The furthest left line is the first time Cherry did the feared activity. The anxiety goes up very high then only slowly drops. The lines to the right represent each subsequent attempt. Every time, anxiety goes up a little less high, and comes down a little more quickly.

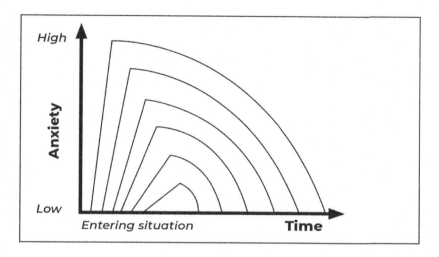

Once you can do the first step, with only a small rise in anxiety, which rapidly drops again, then move onto the next step. In Cherry's case this was getting on.

Getting on caused a huge spike in anxiety. All we did was stand there till the anxiety dropped. Then she got off, had a break and then got back on again. Exactly the same pattern was repeated.

Once getting on was not a problem, we moved onto the next step, and the next, and the next. Ensuring each step was small enough for success, but big enough to generate anxiety.

Simply forcing yourself to take the next step is not enough: it is the anxiety dropping that teaches the

Chimp. Your anxiety needs to be high enough to drop, but not so high that you can't see the process through.

Drawing up Your Hierarchy

Decide in advance what your Steps-To-Success hierarchy looks like:

Step 1

Step 2

Step 3

etc

You can have as many steps as you like as long as you keep moving forward.

Troubleshooting:

This approach works. It can't not. It is simple biology. The body just cannot sustain a state of panic for very long. The anxiety HAS to drop, so your anxiety will come down in the end. Whatever you are doing at that point re-wires the Chimp brain.

Problems arise when:

- You choose a task that does not generate high enough anxiety. The anxiety has to be high enough to drop. You can be a bit worried for hours, but you can't be truly anxious for more than a few minutes.

- You do not allow anxiety to drop but get off before that has happened. This teaches the opposite of what you want. This is the most common reason for the process not to work: The person simply does not see it through. This is why starting at a level you feel you can see through is so important.
- You do not repeat each step often enough. If you move on too fast you are unlikely to habituate properly to any of the steps, and you may well then find yourself giving up because it is 'not working'.
- You leave too long a gap before each repetition. Re-wiring is a process over time, not something that happens immediately.
- You start with too difficult a challenge as this can prevent a person from seeing it through.
- You do not have enough steps in the hierarchy
. You keep having setbacks (see below)
. Your fear is being driven by unresolved trauma (see below)
- Your fear is not irrational (see below)

KEY CONCEPT:
Re-wiring the Chimp brain requires repeated, prolonged exposure to what scares you.

Repeated Setbacks

The Chimp learns through experience. If you have a fall, or a near-miss, it is entirely natural that the next time you come to ride or to repeat whatever you were doing at that time, will generate some anxiety. The Chimp will be suspicious and may present you with reluctance, to encourage you to avoid. If you ignore that and carry on regardless, the Chimp might present you with mental images and ideas relating to the accident to you. Effectively saying 'BAD IDEA! LOOK WHAT MIGHT HAPPEN!'

The Chimp's most recent experience of riding (or of that aspect of riding) is negative, so he is fairly convinced that riding, or that particular task, is a Very Bad Idea. However, if you work through that and have a series of successful rides, the chimp re-evaluates the risk, and calms down.

But what happens if you have – say – 4 good rides and then another fall or near-miss? Chimp was just beginning to get his head round the idea that this is okay after all, and now there is another incident. This shakes his faith once again, and you will need more successful rides to calm him down again.

Obviously, repeatedly falling off is not ideal, but it can happen. Especially if your horse has developed an injury and is escalating behavior. It can take a while before a person realizes there is a physical issue going on, by which time you may have hit the deck a few times over a few months. The human may be reassured that the problem is sorted, and the horse may be behaving beautifully now. So the human thinks the issue is full resolved and does not understand why they are still anxious about coming off. But those reassurances mean nothing to the Chimp. He only learns from experience. You will need a consistent run of successful rides to help him re-evaluate. Just be patient. If you keep at it, and string together 15-20 positive experiences, the Chimp will eventually trust that things are ok now. His survival brain will catch up with your logical brain – which already knows the problem is resolved, and the risks no longer high.

Unresolved Trauma

As described above, most accidents can be frightening or painful at the time, and may lead to a person feeling more anxious afterwards, as their Chimp's dim view of riding is strengthened by evidence of the dangers inherent in the sport. Subsequent successful rides lead to the perception of risk being re-evaluated, and the sense of threat slowly reduces over time. The accident fades into memory, and the person's confidence is restored.

However, if an accident was particularly traumatic, and the person does not deal with the trauma, but shuts down thoughts of the accident and pushes them away, then those memories can remain live and active. It can feel as if the whole event has been frozen in time. When memories are triggered, a person can re-experience elements of the accident in vivid detail. It can even feel as if the awful experiences are being replayed in the present moment. If this is happening to you, the anxiety will not habituate, as those trauma memories are keeping the sense of threat alive.

Evidence of unresolved trauma may include:

- Persistent re-experiencing of elements of the accident when you try and ride
- Unusually vivid recollections, sometimes also including different senses, such as sensations in your body or smells
- Intense emotion when memories are triggered
- A sense that the traumatic incident was very recent, even if it happened years ago
- Avoidance of any reminders of the accident
- Difficulty talking about it, and a wish to push memories away
- A sense of threat/jumpiness
- Irritability and low mood

If you feel you are struggling with unresolved trauma, then you will need to seek support from a mental health professional. It is beyond the scope of this book to address this. Treatment needs to be offered by a properly trained and accredited practitioner. Be very wary of confidence coaches who claim to be able to treat this, unless they have a solid foundation in mental health. Trauma Focused CBT and EMDR are both very effective therapies to help you move past your memories.

To regain confidence, you will need to address trauma memories first, so that the accident fades, and you are no longer experiencing powerfully intense emotional reactions. When that has happened, you can then move forward with graded exposure. Trauma memories can be addressed surprisingly quickly, once you know what the problem is, and engage in an appropriate therapy. I have worked with a number of riders, who are back riding with confidence, after first addressing trauma off the horse.

Is Your Fear Rational?

Occasionally a rider finds themselves with a horse who is more challenging than they can reliably cope with. The horse may be temperamentally too sharp or green for the rider's skill level. The horse may need something from the rider they are not getting, such as clearer direction or confidence. Or the horse may have developed behavioural issues that the rider is struggling to address.

When your horse tanks off with you, your problem is not a fear of riding in open spaces, but perfectly rational recognition that you are unsafe in open spaces. When your horse appears to be taking you to the fence, but then slams on the brakes, your problem is not a fear of jumping, it is a perfectly rational concern about being sent headfirst into a jump.

These may be schooling gaps, or horse confidence issues, and these problems may have arisen, at least partly, due to a rider's own anxiety. But if you are genuinely not safe on your horse, then you need to address the problems with your horse, alongside the issues with your own confidence.

An anxious rider needs to be on a confident and forgiving horse, who will not be upset by a rider's nerves, and who will allow the rider to occasionally balance on their hands, ride a dodgy line, lose balance, or use heavy, unclear or unintended cues, without overreacting to that.

Equally, an anxious horse needs the rider to be positive and confidence giving. Horses are prey animals and are extraordinarily intuitive. They can pick up tension and anxiety, whether expressed physically or emotionally. As discussed earlier, they can tell if you aren't breathing properly, or if a fence is making you nervous. Horses hold their breath to listen out for danger and if one herd member holds their breath, the whole herd can follow suit and become alert and ready for action. If you hold your breath your horse may well assume there is danger around, and become tense and ready for flight. If you then notice this change in your horse, and get even more anxious, the horse will know you are worried about something, but won't have any idea that you are anxious of HER. She will just think 'what's wrong', and react accordingly.

Horses can develop behavioural issues very quickly when inadvertently rewarded by the wrong response. If a horse feels a little reluctant to leave the yard and naps, a rider softening their hands and riding positively forward can nip that in the bud quickly. The horse learns that leaving the yard is no big deal, begins to trust the rider more, and the napping stops. However, if the rider takes their leg off, or decides to get off or turn back, then the horse rapidly learns that the way to stay 'safe' with his pals on the yard is to nap, and things can get worse quickly. Many such 'evasions' are actually learned behaviours that we have trained the horse to use.

If an anxious rider does find themselves on a horse who lacks confidence, or has developed some evasions, or both, then it is useful to work on your own confidence on a school-master, while someone else works with your horse. Especially if your horse is young and green, or is having a problem with something and needs to be helped to understand or gain confidence. In general, you can only proceed at the pace of the weakest link in the partnership. It is important not to get impatient with either yourself or the horse. Things take the time they take. For both of you! Rushing just causes more tension and stress, and in the end, slows progress down.

KEY CONCEPT:
You can only progress at the pace that the weakest link in the partnership feels is safe and manageable.

Summary

This chapter has introduced you to the Circle of Stress and discussed strategies for addressing all 4 quadrants. These, together, lead us to ride in a state of fear: physically tense, psychologically fixated on danger, emotionally vulnerable, and attempting to cope with all that via the Chimp behaviours of flight or freeze.

There are many ways we can help soothe the Chimp, but the crucial step needed for overcoming this brain-based fear is providing the Chimp with new experiences, so he re-evaluates what he considers threatening or dangerous. We have to face our fears to re-wire the brain and truly overcome them.

The Chimp is easily identifiable when he goes into complete meltdown. When the body is in threat mode, the person experiences intense fear, and thoughts spiral into a series of 'what if' catastrophes. In that state, the person may decide not to ride again, or to limit what they are willing to do. He or she will be well aware that this decision is driven by fear. They may like the idea of riding, but are simply too frightened.

However, scaring us into obedient submission is not the only way the Chimp influences our choices. Just as common, and often harder to spot, is his use of Avoidance. This is not the 'Flight' type of avoidance, seen in running away in terror, but the more low-key avoidance that comes from a sense of 'nah'. This reluctance feels like it is arising from your own wishes, and not coming from the Chimp. It is important that we recognize when this is happening so we can address it. I call this 'nah, not really feeling it today' reaction the Chimp's 'Bad Idea, Best Avoided' strategy. This is discussed in Chapter 6 to ensure your decision making is not being hijacked by an upset Chimp.

Once you are actually riding, the Chimp can also hijack you, making you ride in a defensive or passive way, and by making you more error prone by reducing your access to your skills. Chapter 6 gives you the tools you need to not just ride, but to ride *well*.

CHAPTER 6

Soothing an Upset Chimp

Managing 'Bad Idea, Best Avoided' Reactions

Flight mode can trigger emotional meltdown, but that only happens when the Chimp thinks that what you are planning or doing poses a serious and imminent threat to safety, or even survival. However, another very common Chimp strategy, linked to the flight instinct, is avoidance. The Chimp has evolved to spot and avoid problems. He can decide that something is a 'Bad Idea, Best Avoided'. And can train you to believe that his idea is your idea.

You will notice a reluctance to do something (flight), anger with someone for suggesting you do something (fight), or difficulties accessing your skills when trying to do something your Chimp finds worrying, (freeze).

To deal with this, you need to understand what is happening, and then simply, calmly accept it. I call it my 'anywhere but here' feeling. As in I'd rather be anywhere but here, and doing anything but this. Multiple goal medallist and Tour de France winner, Bradley Wiggins, described much the same feeling at the

Olympics. It just means either that the event, goal or challenge matters hugely to you, and you are therefore taking a risk in possibly failing. Or that the task feels daunting and overwhelming.

The Chimp perceives threats in both fear of failure in terms of performance, and fear of failure leading to falls/injury. These apparent dangers trigger the Chimp into asking: 'why, just why?' The Chimp is often sneaky enough not to focus on fear. Instead, the reluctance can be around getting up early, travelling, turning the horse out, packing the lorry etc. Basically, a sense that it is all overwhelming and too much effort, so why bother?

You don't need to waste time trying to answer that question. No answer will satisfy the Chimp, and you, the human, already know the answer. When you are experiencing nerves the night before an event, it can be hard to re-connect with your own motivation, because the Chimp has switched to threat mode and is therefore emotional and not open to reason. You just have to trust that what motivated you to agree to participate in the first place remains valid, and calmly accept that the Chimp disagrees.

I used to try and remind myself of all the reasons I love eventing when I had the 'anywhere but here' feeling. But that conversation became one-sided and circular, as I just didn't believe myself. Or rather, my Chimp did not believe me:

Chimp: Urgh why am I doing this?

K: I love eventing

C: But it's scary and I have to get up at 4:30 in the morning and it's a huge pain

K: I really like eventing

C: Surely I could just do clinics and camps and have fun, instead of putting myself through this all the time.

K: But I want to event

C: WHY though? It takes up the whole day, costs an arm and a leg, is bloody scary. Riding is supposed to be FUN

K: I've already entered. I'm doing it

C: But the money has gone now. I can still pull out and have a nice chilled day instead. The weather looks rubbish anyway. Why put myself through it.

Yada yada yada.

When engaged in an internal argument, it is sometimes useful to ask yourself – who is arguing with who? Usually the human (the authentic I) is arguing with one of the mental menagerie critters. In the case of 'Bad Idea, Best Avoided', it is most likely to be the Chimp.

It is more effective to just notice it, accept it, refuse to argue with it and tell myself 'I'm scared because I care.' Or 'I'm not nervous, I'm excited.' And then to turn my attention to something else, safe in the knowledge that once I am actually doing it, all those fears evaporate.

> **KEY CONCEPT:**
> **The 'anywhere but here' feeling just means the Chimp feels threatened.**
> **Calmly accept and ignore it.**

Fear of Failure

The 'anywhere but here' feeling is the price you pay for the joy of a significant, hard-won achievement. You can't have one without the other. If you care, you will trigger nerves, and if you don't really care, then the outcome won't give you that buzz.

Failure is subjective. I have been ecstatic with 2 cross-country stops (I wasn't eliminated!) And frustrated with a pole when show-jumping when I was hoping for a clear. Most people go into an event with an idea of how they want to do, and a fear that they will not achieve their aims. It is important to remember that the main reason success feels so sweet, is because failure, (however you define that), is so much more common and likely. Especially in horse sport where there are 2 of you able to make a silly or careless mistake. And especially in eventing where there are 3 separate opportunities for both of you to slip up. People can also fear 'failure' regarding what they do with their horse. Avoiding trying to hack out, for fear of the horse napping and refusing to leave the yard. Avoiding a schooling exercise, in case you don't achieve what your instructor was asking for.

Anything that is a genuine challenge for you is also, by definition, something that you may not succeed in. Otherwise it would not be a challenge. If your main struggle relates to competition nerves, or fear of hacking out, then entering levels below what you are capable of at home, or going on a short hack with a foot soldier, make perfect sense. A good performance, or a successful ride out, will still feel satisfying, as in those situations the heights, or technical demands of the tests or hack are irrelevant: The challenge lies in competing or hacking at all, which makes them a significant achievement, regardless of the degree of technical difficulty. In these situations, of course, you will still experience nerves.

On the other hand, if neither you nor the horse need exposure at lower levels or with easier tasks for confidence, does entering classes or practicing skills far below your actual ability, feel satisfying?

The only way to avoid the fear of failure completely is to enter events or try new exercises or outings that are well beneath your actual competency level – both in terms of technical skill and related to fear. This might be less stressful, but is also far less satisfying. If you are realistically capable of far more than you ever try to achieve, do you really feel fulfilled?

It is easy to avoid failure. Just never try anything that is remotely a stretch for you or your horse. But if you want to move forward, you need to try things you may not succeed in. A constructive, positive attitude to errors and set-backs is essential for progress and learning, unlike frustration and dissatisfaction, which are unhelpful. This is discussed in more detail later, when we get to know the Parrot.

Fear of Danger

A different kind of fear is the fear that the challenge is just too big, the jumps too scary. That there is no way your horse can jump them all safely. There is no getting away from the fact that horse riding is dangerous, and eventing particularly so. A healthy respect for solid fences is essential. Recklessness is unsafe and unfair on both you and your horse. Before you start any kind of fast riding, jumping or riding in open spaces, you need to know that you are both competent and capable. Your riding instructor is best placed to advise on that. But if you are riding at an appropriate level for the competition or event you have entered, or indeed any challenge you want to do, like a beach ride or a jump in a lesson, then dwelling on danger stops being healthy, and instead becomes disabling. Therefore your fear actually increases the risk. You can use the strategies outlined in this book to put your Chimp back in his cage, and calm him down, so you can focus on actually riding.

Break the Task Down into Manageable Chunks

Crises of confidence about competing can happen because people start thinking about how huge the task feels. They know they can jump a 90cm table in training. But the idea of jumping 20 efforts in a row seems – well – 20 times harder. But of course it isn't. If you can jump fence 1, then you can jump fence 2. And fence 3.

The simple solution: Stop thinking about the enormity of the task. Break it down in your mind. Just do what you are doing, right now.

This is so simple and yet so effective: If the magnitude of the challenge is threatening to overwhelm you, STAY PRESENT. Think, I'll just walk down to the warm-up and see how I feel. Then I'll just walk and trot around and see how I feel. Then I'll just have a canter and see how I feel. I'll just pop a practice fence and see how I feel. I'll just head for the start-box and see how I feel. I'll just jump fence 1 and see how I feel.

You are only ever jumping one fence at a time and you can always stop. At any time. But if you are focused on right here, right now, you probably won't want to, because the present moment is usually fine. There might be a bigger fence half way round, or a big rider frightener, like a hedge, but there is no point worrying about that fence till you are there. And by then you are likely to be flowing and fine.

This advice is also very helpful for long distance endurance events. Worrying about mile 48 when you are feeling fatigued at mile 12 is overwhelming. But you don't have to run mile 48 when you are running mile 12. You just have to run mile 12. And then mile 13. Sometimes even a mile can feel overwhelming, in which case break the task down even more. Run 100m at a time. Or a single step at a time.

It also applies to life. If you can't face tidying your house, tidy your bedroom. If you can't cope with that, tidy one drawer. Just do *something*, in the direction of your goal. Continuing, once you have begun, it is often much easier than taking that first step.

Mantras I use a lot are 'one step at a time', or 'just start moving'. For example, I recently had a lesson after a fall. It was somewhere new, and I was not sure where I was going. Getting lost, a new trainer, a new venue, bad weather meaning a fresh horse, and a not-quite-recovered sprained ankle that left me feeling vulnerable, were all playing on my mind. The Chimp took a very dim view of the entire plan. I got so bored hearing the same old Chimp-driven conversation about cancelling, that I just said 'start moving.' I was not committed to actually jumping, just to putting on my coat. Then my boots. Then driving to the yard. Then programming the

SatNav. Then loading Lottie. Then setting off, by which time the Chimp had given up and I had a great lesson.

> **KEY CONCEPT:**
> **If the perceived enormity of the task threatens to overwhelm you, break it down in your mind into bite size pieces which feel more manageable.**

Fire up the Chimp

The other way to address fear is to get fired up for the challenge. This is the opposite strategy to the 'I can stop anytime' approach: It's the 'nothing is getting in my way' mindset.

We can use the Chimp's reluctance to power the performance. The Chimp has 3 strategies: The first of these is Flight (avoid). If that fails, he moves to Freeze or Fight. The switch from Flight to Fight is instant. It needs to be, as this is about survival, as far as the Chimp is concerned. If the Chimp is scared, the Chimp is also motivated, and you can use that constructively by getting psyched up.

Harnessing FIGHT allows people to pull out performances that, in retrospect, they find hard to believe they achieved. You can take on so much more when you are fired up. I experienced this myself. I entered a big and technical BE90 and it looked *huge* and very challenging. I got myself totally fired up and attacked the course, going clear. The same venue has a farm ride – a trail with optional jumps of varying heights looping around the perimeter of the site. A few days after the event I went to do that trail ride, intending to enjoy a relaxed afternoon, popping the odd easy log, tyres or brush. The ride was nothing like as challenging as the cross-country course had been. However, at every single fence, I made an excuse for not jumping it:

Don't like the gap underneath
Don't like the take-off or landing
Too skinny
Too downhill
Weird shape
Weird colour

At one point I glanced over at the cross-country course, which was still visible, and saw jumps twice the height of the ones I was now reluctant to take on. I did the entire 7 miles of the farm ride and did not jump a single fence, as I experienced Bad Idea, Best Avoided all the way round it. Not being fired up meant my willingness and ability to jump had evaporated, virtually overnight.

I also experienced Bad Idea, Best Avoided in warm-ups, struggling to jump a small upright literally moments before I knew I needed to go in and jump a full course. Put fence 1 in the warm-up and I would struggle to jump it. Put fence 1 at Fence 1 and it was fine, because the Chimp was pumped up for the round, in a way he simply wasn't for the warm-up.

To cultivate the attitude of 'nothing is getting in my way' and to help get the Chimp enthused, the way you talk to yourself, and how you prepare for the round is crucial.

When I walk a course my thought process is always 'how am I going to jump this'. Not 'help, *how* on earth will I get over *this*' but – literally – 'what *is* the way I am going to ride this.' I choose a line, something to sight, a canter. Then I visualise myself doing it several times, sometimes adding in a trouble-shooting move in my mind's eye, like shutting the door on an inviting run out at a corner, or changing my bat over.

An obvious question with these two opposite approaches is which to use when. When to break the task down into manageable chunks, and reassure yourself that you are only ever doing this one bit of the task; and when to view the challenge as a whole, and fire yourself up to attack everything in front of you.

As ever, trial and error is useful. Try both and see how your Chimp responds. As a rule of thumb, if you are lacking in confidence because of paralysing fear of the risks, then taking it one fence at a time, with no pressure to keep going, is a good option. When the fear is centred around under-performing, then getting fired up is a better option.

I have twin daughters and at one Hunter Trial they each used one of these strategies. One had come off a few times in recent months as her pony had begun to nap and rear – which turned out to be pain related and was unpredictable. She was worried about just getting round safely. The other had a capable pony who was quite quirky. He was capable of winning, but was equally capable of ditching her at the first and galloping back to the lorries. He responded well to positive, attacking riding. Both jumped clear, so both approaches helped them, but if the rider on the quirky pony had tried taking it one fence at a time, then I doubt she would have ridden positively enough to get a clear out of him. Whereas the child who rode one fence at a time had to overcome a little hesitation to leave the start box. After that she could feel that her pony was travelling nicely, and then felt happy carrying on. If she had not had 'permission', in her own mind to stop, the fear of that start box nap would have been overwhelming, and she is likely to have become tense and tight at the very beginning of the course. The wheels could, therefore, have rapidly come off.

Positive Self-Talk

Another useful way of soothing an upset Chimp is to pay careful attention to what you are saying to yourself. Language shapes how we think and feel in quite profound ways. In triathlon training I would be careful to think in language like 'striving' or 'working', not 'suffering' or 'killing myself'.

Researchers in Germany published an article in the Journal, Pain, showing that saying pain-related words stimulates the pain centres of the brain, even when there is no external stimulus. And that the more the pain centres are stimulated, the more pain you experience. The study demonstrated that warning children that this 'might hurt a bit' makes them experience more pain than not saying anything. Words that particularly excite the pain centres include 'gruelling' and 'tormenting'. If you hit hard patches in training or racing, thinking 'this is hurting, I'm really suffering, this hill is gruelling, this race is killing me!' will actually make you experience more pain. The same is likely to be true of language used while riding: words like 'petrified', 'terrified', bricking it' are likely to trigger more anxiety than words or phrases like 'challenging', 'at my limit' or 'working the edge'.

Humans are well equipped to cope with stress. We have evolved to manage it and have in-built resilience systems. But our brains and bodies vary significantly in terms of how we deal with stress, depending on how we view it. Dr Jeff Rediger's best-selling book, Cured, focuses heavily on the mind-body connection. Rediger explains that our nervous system can interpret stress in 2 ways: as a challenge or as a threat. We respond negatively to threat stress and can feel overwhelmed. Whereas we are motivated and energised by challenge stress. Ensure your self-talk and your preparation prime your Chimp for perceiving the task ahead as a challenge, and not as a threat.

> **KEY CONCEPT:**
> **We can use the FIGHT instinct to overcome Flight and Freeze and change our perception of the task from a threat to a challenge.**

PMA Statements

An effective way of utilizing language and self-talk is by using PMA statements. These are statements that you say to yourself before and during riding in order to help you get into the right mindset to be effective. PMA, in sport psychology, usually means Positive Mental Attitude, referring to motivational or aspirational quotes or thoughts. However, it is very important that PMA statements are personally meaningful and unique to you. Generic motivational statements are nowhere near as effective as ones that you develop yourself specifically for each new challenge. I invent different PMA statements for dressage, show-jumping and cross-country; and for schooling, training and competing. I also come up with new ones for every challenge I do.

I think of PMA as standing for Positive/Personal, Motivational/Meaningful and Aspirational/Authentic.

The Positive, Motivational and Aspirational elements get you stoked up. The Personal, Meaningful and Authentic elements ensure that the statement is specific to you, and therefore far more effective.

'What have you done to Katie?' joked the riding instructor. She was on day 2 of a camp and the cross-country lesson on day 1 had not gone well. She had ridden dodgy lines, been a bit passive, and had had some stops and run-outs.

'Can I have a session?' she asked me afterwards. 'I don't want to ride like that tomorrow.'

We spent the afternoon unpicking the ways in which she had ridden and identifying the changes she needed to make: chiefly thinking ahead, being clearer in her own mind about the lines she was going to ride, and then communicating with her pony with more clarity and commitment. Instead of setting off for the line of jumps, headed in vaguely the right direction, and refining the steering en-route to the fence. Before each line, she took a moment to gather her thoughts along with her reins, did a rein back to canter to get the pony 'with' her, and was clear, from the moment she moved, where she was going on the approach and the ride away. She was a quiet rider so that did not need to change. What she needed was more focus and clearer intent, rather than getting more active from the pony's back. She visualized riding positively and the pony flowing and flying. Her PMA statement was 'fire and focus'. The partnership was totally transformed the following day. Her pony felt full of confidence, and Katie ended up riding lines she had never dreamed of jumping. All through changing her mindset.

> **KEY CONCEPT:**
> **PMA statements can get us into the right mindset for effective riding.**

Freeze Mode

In flight mode the Chimp does not want to do it at all. If you successfully manage to calm your Chimp down enough to be able to override the flight instinct, you may then enter 'freeze' mode, where the Chimp can have an attitude of 'ok just get it done quick, then you can get off'. The brain is not focused on riding *well*, but just on getting through it. Ironically, you then are unlikely to ride to your ability. Which will confirm to the Chimp that you should not have been doing it in the first place.

You may also find that you are now riding with an upset Chimp. Unhappy Chimps use freeze mode if they can't run away. 'Freeze' behaviours are a combination of behaviours that occur because you can't think straight, and behaviours the Chimp thinks will keep you safer. The trouble is the Chimp can't ride.

Freeze behaviours include:

- Chucking the reins at the horse as you approach the jump
- Tipping forward (heading for the foetal position)
- Taking your leg off
- Gripping
- Staring at the jump, instead of looking up and ahead
- Sitting passively/being a passenger
- Pulling back on the rein to stop him doing something, or to hang on

In short, the opposite of the positive, effective riding you are capable of. People get very frustrated when they find themselves making the same 'mistake' over and over again, such as taking the leg off or tipping forward. The problem isn't with your riding skills. The problem is that you lose access to your skills if you are riding in Chimp-Mode.

The reality is that the Chimp is 5 times faster and 5 times stronger than the human. If he decides to take over at the last second, you will not be able to over-ride him.

> **KEY CONCEPT:**
> **Mistakes made in 'freeze mode' usually arise**
> **because the rider is struggling to access**
> **their skills**

Common Problems and How to Address Them

Losing Access to Skills

You can help maintain access to your skills by identifying your own freeze behaviours, and then consciously doing the opposite. If you tip forward, think 'sit back'. If you take your leg off and stare at the jump, think 'look up and kick on'. Practice riding with good form over easier fences, and then lock in that feeling and ride towards slightly more challenging fences in exactly the same way. Visualise riding effectively and positively.

Use Anti-Freeze!

Freeze behaviours are instinctive and automatic. They are Chimp driven. As the Chimp is stronger and faster than you are, the only way to prevent them is to outsmart the Chimp. You can't just 'stop' a freeze behaviour. You need to replace it with an 'anti-freeze' behaviour.

If you tend to look down as you approach a jump, it is not helpful to think 'don't look down'. Thinking 'look up' is better, but it is even more effective to focus on something beyond the fence and root your attention to that. This overrides the tendency to look down. If you hang onto the horse's head without releasing, it may help to think 'hands soft' or 'hands forward'. However, at the crucial moment, you may automatically pull back. Instead, do something like slip your fingers under the neck strap. If you fidget and interfere on the last stride to a fence don't just think 'hands still'. Instead think 'press knuckles into base of neck'. Or bridge the reins – do something proactive that you can focus on.

If you have multiple freeze behaviours at the same time, then you may need to repeat a challenge a few times, finding ways to override each one. I found this with my 'bogey fence' – the owl hole. I dislike them which means all my horses naturally do too. (Thanks Chimp). As they do not form part of eventing at my level, I never really felt motivated to deal with my reluctance, but my instructor had other ideas. I avoided that jump for a couple of cross-country lessons, but in the end decided to go for it.

I visualized the line. I focused on looking through the hole at something on the other side. I kept my hand forward and I had a decent canter. But at the last second, I unconsciously took my leg off. Everything else was positive and proactive. But the leg was enough of an 'oh help, please don't jump' cue for my horse to slam on the brakes, sending me through alone. (Sometimes a clever horse can be a curse!) She knew I had stopped saying 'go', so she stopped. However, I presented again and this time I focused on leg, really locking into the feel of that leg supporting her, and thinking 'squeeze off the ground.' She popped through beautifully.

Making Silly Errors

These arise because a person can't think straight due to blood being diverted to the emotion centres, or because a person rushes to get it over with. The Chimp calming strategies discussed earlier can all help with this. Once you are on board, breathing effectively, using the half-smile and sitting in a good posture, you can switch your focus to the task at hand.

Using Speed not Impulsion

A common effect of 'get it over with' thinking is launching your horse at the fence with little thought and less preparation. But you cannot use speed to get over a spooky jump. All speed will do is make any stop much more dramatic. It is far better to come in with the appropriate canter, or even trot, and let your horse see what he's doing.

Lack of Focus

To jump well, the horse needs to be set up well. A rider will ride most effectively if they think through the task, plan how to ride, visualise the line or test movement, select the canter needed and think several steps in advance to prepare the horse. In the case of jumping, you also need to choose what to sight, and plan the ride-away. A Chimp in freeze mode generally does not do this, but focuses on the fence, or the imminent transition or movement. Chimp becomes tunnel visioned and does not focus on the full task, including all the elements that occur before and after the fence or movement.

I experienced this the other day. There was a 'scary' jump and I took a deep breath (tick), used a self-motivating statement (tick), got a good canter (tick), looked over not at the jump (tick), cleared it with ease (tick)… And then nearly rode into a wall because I had not planned beyond just getting over the jump.

You can practice this off the horse too. Imagine a virtual reality headset showing you tackling a cross-country track, negotiating a show-jumping course or riding a dressage test. As the course or test unfolds, practice looking and thinking ahead, and setting your horse up early and well.

Hyper-Focus on the Wrong Things

Feared objects act like giant magnets for your mind. Your emotion brain drags your attention to the thing that is worrying it, and insists you focus on that too. But it is not usually something useful to focus on, as it will be a ditch, or the base of a big fence, or anything else you (Chimp) decides is a potential hazard.

This photo is a clear demonstration of how your horse knows EXACTLY where you are looking.

I was not meant to be jumping that far edge of the 'eye-lash' of course. I was meant to be jumping the low point in the middle of the eye-lash. But the jump looked huge and scary, and I was transfixed – like a rabbit in the headlights – by the highest part of the fence. I brought huge intensity and energy to that line, as I was frozen in fear. My horse, Amber went, 'oh that bit. No problem.' If my instructor had asked me to jump that tiny section of the fence on purpose, I could not have done it in a million years. But a horse knows what line you are seeing, and picks up the intensity of your focus. The more intense you are, the more energised and motivated the horse will be, on the basis that she will assume this really, really matters. So next time your instructor shouts: 'where are you looking' you will know why. And next time you find your eyes drawn to a ditch, remember that whatever you are looking at will be what your horse focuses on too.

The same pattern of looking at the wrong thing is seen in skiers trying to navigate woods, or mountain bikers on rocky descents. It is so easy to concentrate on the trees, when you need to pay attention to the gaps between the trees, or to focus on the rocks or roots you are trying to avoid, instead of on the line you want to ride. If you focus on trees and roots, you are much, much more likely to hit trees and roots. Focusing on what you are actually trying to do, and the lines you want to ski or ride, will give you a much better chance.

'Bogey Fences': Whose Problem are They Really?

'At one point we had 3 horses stuck on top of the island.' John chuckles as he tells the story of the controversial obstacle he built for the cross-country phase of a BE80. From the horse's point of view it was very straight forward. A raised island requiring a step up, couple of strides across it and a simple pop off. But there was a ditch all around the base of the island so the simple step turned into a step-with-ditch on both the up and the down elements. The horse would not normally even notice that. But the riders certainly did.

'The first time the island appeared it led to a near mutiny among riders,' continues John. 'I can't tell you how many complaints there were.' And the island caused huge problems out on course. Were those riders right? Was it an unfair question?

John decided to experiment. After the island he build a pair of tricky skinnies. And at the event where they first appeared, the riders started worrying about the skinnies, and their focus shifted away from the island. 'Guess what,' he concludes, 'the island did not cause any problems anymore when the skinnies were there.' However, crucially, in future events without the skinnies, the island once again became problematic.

The message is clear. The horses did not have an issue with the island, the riders did. As soon as the course builder gave them something else to worry about, their focus shifted away from the island and those problems evaporated. But recurred when the island again became the focus of concern for riders.

Summary

We will all be very familiar with making the same mistakes over and over again. This can be extremely frustrating, and riders often believe they need to try harder and practice more. Effort and practice are important, but in the case of looking at the base of the fence, or taking the leg off on the approach to the jump, or riding a poor line to a corner, the issue is not a lack of skill. The solution is not to try harder and repeat the task (and most likely the mistake) over and over. It is to recognize that you have been hijacked by an unhappy Chimp, and are not able to access your skills.

You therefore need to find ways to prevent that Chimp hijack, so that you can use the skills you already have. This chapter gives you plenty of ideas to try. See what works best for you.

A Work in Progress

Chimp taming is not something you can do once and then forget about. It is like physical fitness – use it or lose it. The more you use Chimp taming and soothing strategies, the more manageable and calm your Chimp will be. But if you stop using them, then he will regain a foothold in your mind and become overly influential again. It is a constant process which needs to become an integral part of your riding. We can understand why this is so, by thinking about what is actually happening at a brain level, when your Chimp interferes with your goals and plans.

Take 2 groups who are as happy, chilled and functional as each other. Who, if asked, would say something like 'you know I'm pretty cheerful. I feel good about myself, and life is just fine, thanks.'

One group of people have never been depressed. The others have recovered from depression. Let's stick them in a room, play funereal music at half-speed in the dark, and make them think sad thoughts. Not surprisingly, they feel glum and down afterwards. Then ask them why they feel sad.

Group A will say 'well obviously, because you've played slow sombre music to me in a dark room while making me think sad thoughts. Duh.' The other group will say 'well it's because I'm worthless and useless, and my life is terrible and I'll never achieve anything.'

This is the pattern identified by a famous experiment which highlighted differences between recovered-depressed people, and people who had never been depressed. Most of the time the recovered-depressed and never-depressed groups functioned as well as each other, and were as happy and relaxed as each other.

However, the experiment showed that under certain conditions, old neural chains, and old patterns of thought can be reactivated.

Depressed people have a constant stream of negative thoughts about themselves, the world and the future running through their minds. These thoughts get repeated so often they eventually form part of the brain's neural circuitry. You literally hardwire chains of negative thoughts into your brain. Once a person has recovered, these can lie dormant and inactive for years. However, they can be triggered under certain conditions, and so recovered-depressed people can be vulnerable to accessing these chains again.

This is related to another process called 'mood congruent memory'. When you are cold you can't imagine being hot and vice versa. When we are scared and feel incompetent, we just can't recall what it feels like to feel self-assured. We can remember what we did, but it's much harder to recapture how we felt.

This is relevant to riding as the same processes can arise. If you have ever lost confidence then you have created those neural networks, even if you have regained confidence. You can silence them, you can switch them off, but you can't erase them completely. It is important to understand and accept this calmly. Don't think of it in terms of 'never getting over it'. If the chains are inactive then you *are* over it in the sense that these patterns no longer affect you. However, when they are briefly reactivated, it is helpful to recognise that your brain can give you incorrect and unhelpful information, and you do not need to accept this information as true.

It is common for me to work with someone who is doing really well. Then Life Happens, riding takes a back seat, and anxiety creeps back in. Due to the processes discussed above people don't say: 'I'm feeling a bit nervous because I've not ridden recently, and the Chimp needs to be reminded that there is no problem. No big deal.' Instead people say: 'I'm scared, I know I'll never be able to ride confidently.'

If I point out that not 3 weeks ago they *were* riding confidently, they say 'oh I've no idea how I did that!'

The good news is that you can regain confidence very quickly, as long as you simply accept that it has dipped because you have not been able to ride consistently, instead of telling yourself you are back to square one. The more often you feel worried, and then regain confidence, the quicker it will happen and the longer you can leave it between sessions to maintain it. To start with, sessions need to be very regular.

When you are scared and feeling incompetent, it's hard to recapture what self-assurance feels like. If we allow our current emotional state to dictate what we believe about ourselves and our riding, then this temporary anxiety and self-doubt will feel insurmountable. We believe that because we can't imagine feeling confident then we can't ever feel that way. But this is simply untrue. You can be terrified, do it anyway, re-educate the Chimp, and then wonderful confidence comes flowing back. If you understand this then you can just stop worrying about it and use a phrase like 'I know I can do it because I've done it!' This can be very effective in silencing that voice that says 'you'll never be able to....'

> **KEY CONCEPT:**
> **Avoidance of riding can lead to anxiety creeping back in. Calmly expect and accept this. As soon as you get back on it, your confidence will grow again.**

A Credibility Issue

For several years after overcoming my fear of jumping I needed to jump regularly to stay confident. I used to find that the first 5 or so jumps in every jump lesson were a bit nerve wracking, but then I'd settle. Slowly that turned to the first 2-3 jumps. Then even that stopped, as long as I jumped every week. I was eventually able to stretch it out to 10 days, then 2 weeks without reactivating the neural 'oh help' chains.

Unfortunately, Amber got injured, and I did not jump for months. Eventually she retired and I started viewing other horses, with the hope of eventing with them. I had, unfortunately, forgotten that jumping was going to be a problem.

One embarrassing afternoon unfolded thus:

I was trying out a nice mare, having explained that I wanted a horse for BE90/100. The flat work was fine but, of course, event horses have to jump. Ah.....There was already a course laid out in the arena.

'Erm can I just have a cross-pole?' I asked.

Sure,' said the seller, perhaps thinking I was just getting warmed up. I headed towards it. At this point 2 parallel realities unfolded.

In MY reality, the horse bolts towards the fence, balloons it, stumbles on landing and almost ditches me. I cry, and say I don't want to jump anymore.

In the real world, (as evidenced by the video that was kindly, but rather humiliatingly, being taken), the horse takes me to the fence with a slight increase in pace, jumps it perfectly normally, if a little enthusiastically, and then slightly pecks on landing. If you are looking very closely.

Our 2 worlds re-converge with the crying and wanting to get off bit.

The seller clarified, 'so this is a horse you plan to event?'

'Yes.'

'With YOU riding her?!'

Oh dear. We left. And after that, my daughters did the jumping at viewings.

Once I had my new horse, though, I was fine. I knew what to do, and I did it. I started at cross-poles and accepted the discomfort needed to re-train the Chimp. We are now jumping as confidently as I ever did with Amber. I have now overcome jumping nerves so often that I can have a lengthy break, or a fall, and still be able to start back at more or less the level I finished on.

If you have a wobble you are not back at the very beginning. You just need to put what you have learned into practice, and crack on again. Every time you repeat the process of moving past a wobble, you weaken anxious neural chains, you strengthen confident neural chains and you re-educate the Chimp a little bit more. Each time, the process is faster, and you get back to where you left off quicker than before. But you do have to do the work.

Most importantly, you need to focus on Chimp taming without 'help' from the that critical voice inside your head, who will try and tell you that you are back to square 1, that you will never get anywhere, that your riding is embarrassing, that you are a total idiot for repeating mistakes etc etc. Time to explore that voice in more detail. Let's meet the Parrot.

CHAPTER 7

The Pesky Parrot

Imagine you have always dreamed of owning a talking parrot. You save up for months and one day, excitedly, you decide that you can now afford one. You hurry to the pet shop. All the parrots are asleep but the shopkeeper points out a lovely looking bird.

'It definitely talks?' you ask anxiously.

'Oh yes, you can't shut it up once it it's awake,' says the shopkeeper.

You hand over your hard-earned cash and head home, looking forward to hearing what it has to say later on.

Then it wakes up and you discover that this particular parrot has been trained to pass negative, critical commentary on you and your life. All. Day. Long.

Those runners stressed about being slow? – Parrot.

Those athletes feeling out of place and self-conscious? – Also Parrot.

This parrot is just a parrot. It doesn't have any knowledge, wisdom or insight. It's bird-brained after all.

It recites things 'parrot fashion', without any understanding or comprehension.

How long would you put up with this abuse before throwing a towel over the cage, or getting rid of that pet-shop parrot?

Yet when we hear those same voices of criticism and negativity inside our own heads, we can often struggle to see this as an unhelpful process, reciting nonsense, parrot-fashion. It becomes internalised. It becomes us. This is our Parrot. And we can put up with this internal bully for far too long. We can spend decades or a lifetime tolerating this Parrot in our minds.

We hear our 'Parrot', believe its words, and naturally get upset. That then affects the way we live our lives: the way we behave towards others, what we think about them, what we think about the world, and how we think and feel about ourselves.

I am not immune to the Parrot. In fact, in another one of those moments where I realised that me the psychologist is not really any different to me the human, it was treating depressed adolescents that helped me conceptualise the constant stream of negative thinking in depression as a malevolent talking parrot. But having done so, I became much more aware of 'Parrot-speak' in my own life. We all have a Parrot. This is not unique to people in mental distress but is universal. The Parrot in depression may be more vitriolic or more malevolent, but we all have a Pesky Parrot that affects us to some extent.

What I used to see as *my* lack of self-belief, *my* insecurity was relabelled as 'Parrot FM'. A tedious commentary that I could not switch off completely, but could simply ignore.

This Parrot has no knowledge, wisdom or insight. It is simply trained to provide a constant negative commentary on me and my life. Naming it and seeing it as NOT ME, but just as old, redundant neural circuitry, that bores me, and has no relevance to my life, helps me avoid identifying with the thoughts, or believing them.

> **KEY CONCEPT:**
> **Those voices of negativity and self-criticism and neither YOU nor TRUE.**

The ferocity of the thoughts is sometimes quite shocking once you start paying attention:

When I was training for an ironman a typical pattern would go:

Parrot: 'you'll never be an ironman, you're a joke'

Me: 'whatever'

Parrot: 'And you hate cycling anyway, why do you even want to do an ironman'

Me: 'blah, blah'

Parrot: 'This ride is too hard for you. You're too weak'

Me: 'You're boring me, Go away'

Parrot slopes off in a huff and I finish my ride. No drama, no problem.

However, if I was feeling a bit more vulnerable, for whatever reason, I could let my guard down and start believing that what the Parrot is saying was true. In which case my turbo ride would go something like:

'Parrot: 'Look at your power data. You're a joke. You are so weak and feeble'

Me: 'Oh no, that data is hopeless'

Parrot: 'You'll never be an ironman'

Me: 'Yeah I mean who am I trying to kid'

Parrot: 'So this ride is a pointless waste of time'

Me: 'why am I bothering' (gets tearful)

Parrot: 'Look at you, blubbing because you're a rubbish bike rider. Boo Hoo'

Me: 'I need to stop. This is too hard. I hate it and I hate myself for being such a self pitying loser'

If, at that point, I got off the bike, that would mean:

1) I was paying attention to the Parrot
2) I was identifying with the Parrot
3) I was believing what the Parrot was saying
4) I was therefore obeying the Parrot.

All of which are very unhelpful things to do. Identifying with the Parrot and believing the abuse makes you miserable, unconfident, ashamed and anxious. Obeying the Parrot confirms that it was accurate in how it described you and your life. Thus it becomes a self-fulfilling prophesy. A bullying voice tells us we can't do something. So we don't do it. Then the voice says: 'See! Told you so.'

Luckily it is possible to learn to become aware of this process and simply refuse to indulge the Parrot. To catch the thoughts and turn your attention away. No need to argue back, no need to explain. Just let it go.

There are various mantras you can use in such situations: I often just mentally shout: STOP PAYING ATTENTION TO THIS RUBBISH! And when the Parrot pipes up again, I repeat, simply, ENOUGH! (Zen isn't always very, well, Zen-like).

Stop Drop Breathe

A useful exercise in Parrot-shooting is the Stop Drop Breathe exercise. The first step is to notice you are beginning to identify with Parrot-speak. At that point STOP! Take a step back, mentally and just pay attention to what you are telling yourself. You are essentially creating a story. A narrative about not being good enough, or a failure, or an impending disaster. DROP the story. Don't argue with the story, don't engage with it in any way. Just drop it. And finally BREATHE mindfully to reconnect yourself to reality.

5,4,3,2,1

Another similar exercise also involves noticing Parrot-speak and dropping the story. Then the mindfulness exercise is to look around and identify:

5 things you can see
4 things you can hear
3 things you can touch
2 things you can smell
1 slow deep breath.

You can do this on a horse. Just make sure the 5 things you can see are not things like 'that scary hedge, that pheasant my horse will spook at, my death grip on the reins.' In other words, make sure you don't let the Parrot sabotage the exercise. This exercise involves several senses and can be very grounding.

Shutting up the Parrot is a Choice!

Those exercises are all helpful, but the underlying strategy is making a choice that you will simply not let this voice of misery and criticism define you anymore. Indulging the Parrot is a choice. It does not feel like one, but it is. Almost every time I have a lesson, I hear Parrot conversations around me. And until fairly recently I still engaged in them myself. The more extreme examples of Parrot-abuse I gave earlier were from iron distance training, and I no longer tolerate that kind of internal bullying, thankfully. Training for the iron distance event was more-or-less a 2 year exercise in Parrot-shooting, and I have managed to maintain my discipline around not letting it get a foothold in my mind again. But even while riding, Parrot did sometimes rear its ugly head in more subtle ways.

I had one final story I struggled to overcome. My horse, Amber, was an incredible event horse. She had come to me as a dealer swap for a horse I had to send back, and was sold from the field. She was well-bred but that meant nothing to me. She was grumpy, skinny and there was still just a foal number in her passport. This made me think she must not have much going for her, as she had reached the age of 6 without anyone actually caring about her enough to even name her. I was upset and annoyed that the horse I had originally bought was not fit for purpose and my plan was to get the newly named Amber back into work, sell her on as soon as possible, and then get my 'proper' horse. Which just shows that I am clueless, as she turned out to be fabulous. Incredibly bold and scopey with a great work ethic.

She was certainly not the perfect match for a very average and not terribly brave rider. In that first year, one trainer at a camp told me I was over-horsed, while another offered to buy her. But I absolutely adored her and, although her exuberance was a bit much at times, and she did (literally) ping me out of the saddle once when she ballooned a 60cm fence, I just could not imagine not having her in my life. She never misbehaved. As I explained earlier, she was just a Ferrari for a rider who would have been better off with a Ford. It was up to me to find a way to ride her power. And I did pretty much get to grips with her in the end.

The biggest issue I had was the constant fear that I would be judged as an 'all the gear and no idea' rider. Someone who has gone out and spent mega-bucks on a talented event horse I can't ride, and who I will only ever bimble around 80/90 on anyway.

This fear was magnified at my first riding camp with her when I overheard someone say 'X bought that horse in the end, and she only wants to do BE100. What a waste of a talented horse.' At that point I was aspiring to one day do a BE80, and even that felt a long way off.

I had pre-committed to a camp for aspirational riders, with 5* Event rider and Olympian, Gemma Tattersall. I had checked before booking that the camp accepted all levels. I felt and feel that ambitious riders at 70cm benefit just as much from expert tuition as anyone else. It seems I was alone in that assessment, however, as I ended up having private lessons for the whole camp, because no other riders jumping smaller heights had booked on.

I felt hopelessly outclassed and over-horsed, and felt that I would be judged. So much so, that I actually drove home every night, rather than facing the perceived judgement of my fellow campers. Gemma, however, was absolutely lovely and extremely encouraging. She was the perfect coach for a rider like me: over-horsed but determined to make it work, as she had the expertise I needed.

I was comfortable in my own mind with what we were doing, and how we were progressing. I continued taking lessons with fantastic coaches, and seeking out rich learning opportunities. But the fear of other people's judgements lasted for far too long, not just at camps but in every lesson.

I (Parrot) felt compelled to repeatedly apologise for the horse I was on. The 'tell me about your horse question' was always my opportunity to explain: 'she-was-a-dealer-swap-sold-from-the-field-and-she's-way-too-much-for-me-really-but-I-love-her-so-I'm-trying-to-learn-to-ride-her-better-and-maybe-one-day-unless-you-think-it's-an-insane-idea-I'd-like-to-event-her-at-80-or-maybe-70-maybe'. Deep breath…. Phew.

And one day I decided enough. I belong on her. I do not need to apologise for being on her. I am just going to drop that story. It's irrelevant to what I want to get out of the lesson, it is unhelpful, it is destructive. So stop. Just stop. Now.

I literally had to write a script for myself and mentally rehearse it right before each lesson started. But I did. I walked into the arena on my horse, head up, projecting a confidence I certainly did not feel, and said: 'this is Amber, she is a very onward, bold horse, so I'd like some help with rideability, as we plan to event and I need more control.'

No more information required. I can't tell you how hard that felt. But I was determined that I would never ever again indulge the Parrot's insistence that I would be judged, and needed to pre-empt that with an apologetic spiel and a detailed story. Maybe some people did judge me. So what?

Shooting the Parrot is a choice. So why don't people make that choice?

- They don't separate themselves from the Parrot
- They struggle to take personal responsibility for cultivating a positive mindset
- They have been conditioned to see self-criticism as the path to self-improvement
- They are pre-empting other people's judgements
- Habit
- A form of reassurance seeking
- A reverse sort of arrogance

Not Separating Yourself from the Parrot

The I and the Eye

There is a difference between thinking, and the process of observing your thoughts. It is common to assume that whatever thoughts are in your head are YOU, and for there to be little or no separation between the I who is thinking, and the thoughts themselves.

We can identify fully with that internal monologue, assuming it provides us with a rational reflection of reality. When in fact it does nothing of the sort. Our thinking can be highly distorted, and related to our emotional state, level of physiological arousal, and our brain health. If we are tired, hungry, angry or over-whelmed we will perceive situations very differently from when we are relaxed, happy, calm, well-nourished and well rested.

Imagine you are in a jumping lesson and your horse keeps stopping at a particular fence. The instructor asks you to present again a couple of times, but your horse still won't jump. So she takes the back rail off. Horse is still not happy so she separates the fillers to create a gap. Nope. Then she lowers the height of the fence. Your horse jumps and the instructor rebuilds the fence, adding back in one element at a time. This works well, and after a few minutes you jump the oxer at the original height with the filler. Hurrah, success! But you are thinking 'oh my god I'm so useless. Everyone must be so annoyed about waiting. I should never have come into this lesson.'

It is easy to assume that those thoughts reflect reality. That you *are* useless. That you *are* in the wrong group. That people *are* annoyed. That your emotion-driven, unexamined thoughts are true. But thoughts are not facts. They are just ideas that your brain presents to you, that may or may not have any relationship to reality.

What is actually happening is that 'I am useless and in the wrong group and people are angry' thoughts are arising in your mind. You can notice them and decide whether or not they are accurate or helpful. Or whether they are a distracting irrelevance.

You could just as easily be thinking something a bit more neutral: 'It's awkward that it has taken a bit of time, but at least she jumped in the end.' Or more positive: 'I'm so glad I came as I am learning how to manage her stopping. I am pleased I am getting help with this.'

We spend most of the time in 'I' mode. Just thinking. Not stepping back from our thoughts to consider whether they make any sense, or are helpful to us. We need to spend more time in 'eye' mode. Observing our own thinking and choosing whether to go with these thoughts, to turn our attention away from them or to actively write a new script for the situation. Psychologists call this process 'reframing'.

Accepting Parrot speak as true, and beating ourselves up, means that we fail to appreciate the positives in the situation. For example, that the horse has had her understanding increased by breaking the task down into smaller steps. And that the horse succeeded in the end, and was able to finish on a good note, with restored confidence. Instead, we view the situation negatively and we feel bad. We may look frustrated and upset, rather than focused and interested, so we make the instructor feel bad too. From her point of view, she has successfully helped you manage an issue, and got you jumping something that your horse previously had a problem with. She could well be very pleased with what she considers a job well done. She would be much happier with that outcome if you seemed pleased about it too, rather than embarrassed and upset. We may keep apologizing to the other riders, which also makes them feel bad. And we don't save any time by being upset about taking up time, so it does not help the other riders anyway, even if they *are* annoyed. Which they probably aren't because a good instructor might take 5 minutes with one person to address an issue, but then that person sits out for a little while and the others have their needs addressed. Plus, many riders find that seeing how an instructor goes about addressing a problem is a good learning experience for them.

If we recognize that our thoughts are unhelpful, and often untrue, we can choose to disengage and/or reframe. We can actively turn our attention away from the 'I'm wasting everyone's time' story and embrace an 'I'm glad I'm getting help with my horse' story instead.

The habit of observing thinking is incredibly useful. Especially when much of the stream of consciousness negativity bubbles away at barely conscious level. We can just hear whispers of 'useless, rubbish, won't work', which we are only dimly aware of, but which leave a strong emotional residue. Like toxic glue inside our brain, which bogs us down in negativity and self-criticism.

Parrot FM/Talk to the Hand

If we decide the thoughts are inaccurate, unkind, unhelpful, untrue or abusive, then we can choose to disengage. I use the metaphor of Parrot-FM. A radio playing nonsense in the background. We may not be able to turn it off completely, but we can decide not to pay any attention to it. This takes determination and discipline. I sometimes actually say STOP out loud, when my thoughts are becoming particularly irrational or hysterical. I might even raise a hand while saying STOP, as in 'talk to the hand, I'm not listening to any more of this.'

Reframe

Actively look for the positives or the learning points in any situation. Ask yourself what you would say to a good friend who was in your situation. We are likely to find it much easier to come up with a more balanced and positive perspective, if we view the situation without the distorting effect of Parrot.

A simple example of this is how a rider might think about being a 'happy hacker'. Do you describe or think of yourself as *just* a happy hacker, which devalues the skill and joy of this popular equestrian activity? Or can you be excited and proud of what you achieve in the great outdoors? Do you have the sense that you are wasting your horse? Or are you able to embrace the joy and partnership of hacking adventures with your best friend?

Far too many people appear apologetic about making the choice to hack, rather than school, jump or compete. Yet hacking requires very high levels of skill to negotiate hazards that are often very unpredictable. A friend calls herself a performance trail rider. I love that!

Personal Responsibility

Most people assume their thoughts, feelings and beliefs are driven by external factors.

Steven Bartlett of *'Diary of a CEO'* podcast fame, and the TV programme, *Dragon's Den*, tells the story of how he once tweeted 'X pissed me off.' He then corrected himself to 'I have pissed myself off because of X.'

This closely relates to the Dilts framework outlined in Chapter 2, used in NLP. Saying 'x pissed me off' suggests you are operating at the level of the environment: This happened and this caused this. As discussed earlier, this is a superficial level of processing, and those who operate here tend to be highly influenced by external events and other people. It is far more effective and emotionally mature to take personal responsibility for your own well-being, and to understand that it is usually not the events that cause upset, but the reaction to those events. As Shakespeare said: 'There is nothing either good or bad but thinking makes it so.'

Bartlett explained that he watches his Twitter numbers closely, and lost thousands of followers by taking personal responsibility for how he felt, instead of blaming environmental factors.

It is an unpopular message as people prefer to blame issues outside of themselves for any distress or problems they have. But it is actually a hugely empowering message. If external events are at fault for how you feel, react and behave, then you have no control. If you accept responsibility, then you take back control.

One of Bartlett's most popular guests on the Podcast was Happiness Guru, Mo Gawdat. Mo defines happiness or success as being minimally related to the event itself, and much more to the perception of the event, and to the gap between perception and expectation. Steven Bartlett said that many more thousands of followers would unfollow at that message too. It is hard to accept personal responsibility for your progress, or lack thereof. Much easier to blame other factors: NOOOOO, they are richer, with a better horse, more support, a less demanding job, braver, more talented, better trainers etc. *That's what makes them successful.'*

By all means make sure that your horse is suited to your goals, that your goals are suited to your horse, that you have trainers you trust, that you prioritise work-life balance etc. But beyond that, you hold the cards. Success, (however you personally define it), is a choice. It is perfectly possible to 'win' dissatisfied or 'lose' happily.

Once you are ready to accept that your mindset is not a gift from the gods, but a skill to cultivate, and if you accept personal responsibility for growth and change, then you will begin to make much more progress. And crucially you will *feel* like you are making much more progress.

Fake it Till you Make it

There are strong brain-body links. If you act confidently, you eventually feel more confident. If you act happy, you eventually feel happier. All emotions come with associated 'action urges'. This is because emotion is biological, and aids survival. Anger makes us want to confront and hit out. Anxiety makes us want to avoid or run away. Disgust makes us want to recoil. In this way, if we have spent 3 days tracking a deer to feed ourselves and our family, we will get angry if someone walks over to take it off us. We will fight and defend our food, territory and family, and thus enhance the chance of survival. We avoid danger through anxiety and we avoid disease through disgust.

Emotions involve bodily reactions as well as action urges. With anger we feel hot and tense, as our muscles get flooded with blood, and adrenaline spikes, preparing us to fight more ferociously. With anxiety we shake and hyperventilate, and our heart rate goes up as we increase the oxygen pumping round our system, ready to run away faster. With disgust we feel sick or may retch to avoid toxins or expel them from our body.

'Fake it till you make it' makes use of the fact that we can actually alter our emotional state, by acting as if we are feeling a different emotion, ie: by soothing our body and acting opposite to the instinctive urges. When managing anger it helps to take a deep breath, unclench our fists, shake out tension and splash water on our face. To literally 'cool off'. And instead of shouting or hitting out, we can speak calmly, keeping our body posture neutral, rather than aggressive, and approaching in a conciliatory, rather than a confrontational way. This helps our anger to dissipate. We can regain control of our breathing, and make a conscious choice not to avoid, in order to reduce our anxiety, and feel more relaxed.

By reversing the bodily reaction, and acting opposite to the behavioural urges, we slowly move from faking a sense of calm or confidence, to actually feeling calmer and more confident. This is so effective at changing emotion that 'Opposite Action' is a key tool in the Emotion Regulation modules of therapies designed to enhance our emotion regulation skills and prevent self-harm or suicide.

Staying Present: Mindfulness

Mindfulness is defined as present moment awareness, without judgement. The Parrot, however, epitomizes judgements. All the Parrot does is judge. Judging can be past oriented: 'You idiot what did you do that for!', or future oriented: 'everyone is going to laugh at you. You are going to mess that up.' Parrot can also be found in the present, in the form of critical self-consciousness: 'this is so embarrassing, I am riding like a lemon, I must look like a total idiot right now.'

Mindfulness provides a way of disarming the Parrot. Parrot-Speak is simply regarded as pointless noise. You notice you have disappeared into your head, and started identifying with the noise, and you calmly disengage. Just turn your attention away from that pointless conversation, and focus on what is really happening in the real world. No need to argue with the Parrot. As a rule of thumb, if you would not say it to a friend, don't say it to yourself. If the conversation seems judgemental, or based on past or future, then it is Parrot, and not helpful.

The tennis player, Johanna Konta, was considered to be mentally weak, and struggled with on-court melt-downs. She was stuck around 150 in the world. However, over time, she became one of the most poised, mentally strong athletes on the tour, ending up in the top 10. She credits her transformation to mindfulness: The ability to stay in the moment, just 1 shot at a time, letting go of regret over a poor shot, letting go of worries about a big shot, letting go of frustration over a bad line call. All of that pointless noise gets in the way of peak performance. Instead, she learned to stay calmly present, one shot at a time.

Mindfulness leads to emotional neutrality, in which you drop stories about what is happening, and instead clearly see what actually *is*, not what you are projecting. This emotional neutrality is not just better for us, it is also greatly preferred by our horses. Horseman, Mark Rashid, talks of the value martial arts have brought to his horsemanship by allowing him to cultivate a 'mind little still water', or 'mizu no kokkoro' – a state where the mind is not preoccupied by thoughts and emotions. This is invaluable for building a closer connection to your horse. I experience this directly when I work therapeutically with horses. Clients who bring a spiky energy to the sessions find the horses simply don't want to be near them. Other clients, who allow themselves to be soft and open, find those same horses follow them around, seeking closeness.

Mark Rashid and Jim Masterson explore the transforming effects of letting go of narratives, to see things clearly, as they are, in their award-winning documentary, A Mind Like Still Water.

If Mindfulness is so effective, why do we cling to these self-critical narratives. What do we believe they achieve for us?

Self-Criticism as the Path to Self-Improvement

Some people believe that being hard on ourselves is the only way to get better. That nit-picking and fault-finding will somehow lead to improvements. But does this really work?

Imagine we turn up for a taster session at a local tri club run by a coach. Let's call him Coach A. Coach A looks us up and down with an expression of withering contempt.

'Erm I am here for a work out' you say. 'I want to do a triathlon one day.'

'What you?!' he snorts derisively. 'What experience do you have?'

'Well none actually. But I think it looks fun and a great challenge,' you say, beginning to feel like this was a terrible idea.

'FUN?' he exclaims. 'It's hard work. You need DEDICATION and FITNESS. I don't think it's for you.'

'Why not?' you ask bravely.

He replies with a list:

1) You are overweight
2) You are unfit
3) You are too old
4) You look clueless

Sounds ridiculous? I doubt many coaches talk to potential clients like that, but *this is how we talk to ourselves!*

We DO tell ourselves we are too fat, too unfit, too old and too clueless to be taken seriously. How is that ever going to be the route to achieving anything?

If anyone outside our own minds talked to us like this we would be indignant, if not infuriated. In fact, I entered my first marathon because someone did actually say, 'What YOU?' to me when I suggested I wanted to do one. To be fair to him, I had just finished a hilly half marathon, the Great North Run, in an incredibly slow time, and looked like I was about to expire. But even so, my indignation was such that I did the London Marathon a few months later. And went on to do over 20 more, including hilly off road events. And then progressed to ultra-marathons. When I was preparing for those, I would cover marathon distances or longer, just on training runs. My longest continuous run stands at 76 miles. And I was fired up to one day complete a 100 mile ultra, till injury ended my running dreams. So YES ME, you arrogant sod!

But I would ask myself 'WHO ME?' constantly, right up to the time I actually did one.

There are some Sergeant Majorish coaches out there who believe that the best route to improvement is to be abusive and bullying. The 'chuck 12 eggs at a wall to find the one that doesn't break' approach to coaching. But I think the 11 broken eggs represent a tragic waste of potential. And the one who refuses to buckle under the pressure is probably so driven that they would have been successful anyway. I would not choose to work with Coach A so I refuse to put up with him inside my own head.

Pre-empting Other People's Judgements

Another reason people are self-critical is that they imagine they are already being criticized, and so they pre-empt that by getting your own judgements in first. The main problem with doing this is that you are essentially mind-reading. You have absolutely no idea what other people are thinking about you. And even if people are judging you, so what? I love the quote: 'other people's opinions of you are none of your business.'

My Parrot-Speak centred on fear of other people's judgements, and an associated sense of not belonging, for far too long.

A blog post in December 2018 highlights this:

I recently had a lesson with Nicola Wilson, eventer extraordinaire. During it we had to canter a bend over a pole, get straight to a set of canter poles and ride another bend to finish. Amber maintained balance on the bend and popped through the poles in a lovely rhythm and with good athleticism.

"You enjoyed that didn't you" said Nicola. I beamed in response. But then my bubble was burst....

"You were enjoying your moment of triumph so much that you forgot to ride the 2nd bend" she said.

She was absolutely lovely, and could not have been kinder or gentler in her feedback, but she was spot on. I was stuck on being pleased with myself and literally forgot to keep riding.

*Reflecting on the lesson I realised this is a problem I have a lot of the time. Frankly I find myself so surprised to be doing it at all, that I don't realistically aspire to do it **well**.*

This attitude has been with me all my life. I did an iron-distance triathlon in 2011, and chose to do it on a bright pink bike complete with a set of pink furry dice. This was partly because I like pink. But a more subtle message to the world was 'I am not really taking this too seriously'. Which is nonsense. No-one trains that hard, for that long, to do something that challenging, without taking it seriously! And it is also pointless because frankly The World has better things to worry about than what colour bike I ride. Or indeed whether I complete an ironman or fail to get round.

In retrospect I can see this as a defence against failure. If I make light of the event, keep my expectations firmly in check, and ride a silly looking bike, then perhaps falling flat on my face won't hurt so much?

The trouble is that I have internalised this expectation to fail. I ride dressage tests hoping to avoid mistakes instead of riding to demonstrate Amber's balance, rhythm, straightness or accuracy. I ride fences thinking 'phew' after every fence instead of focusing on the one coming up. And, as I did in the lesson with Nicola, if I ever do something well, I am so surprised at myself that I inevitably fluff the next bit.

I simply don't believe I belong in the eventing world at all, never mind on the podium. Last season I never plaited up. At the time I believed this was because I can't plait for toffee and figured bad plaits look worse than no plaits. But I could **learn** to plait. So perhaps subconsciously my au naturel look is the horsey equivalent of the pink fluffy dice. My tacit acknowledgement that I know I don't belong here, so I need not look the part.

My friend is the opposite. She comes from the background of elite sport and no matter what she enters she is riding to win. Even if the idea of winning that particular event is bordering on delusional. But it makes her 100% more focused and positive in her riding than I am.

This attitude affects everything about my riding. Amber oozes class and credibility in precisely the ways I do not. I never set out to buy a horse like Amber and would not have dared have her had I known how good she is. But why not? After all plenty of riders buy fantastically well-bred horses with great ability and I don't judge them for that. But I have spent 2 years believing I am not a good enough rider for Amber. Believing she is wasted with me, is far too good for me. I adore Amber and she is with me for life so I accepted long ago that I had a responsibility to learn to ride her. But actually it goes further than that. I need to accept that she and I are partners. That I DO belong with her and on her. I DO belong at One Day Events. We are not just making up the numbers while enjoying a nice day out, but are there to compete for placings.

I work hard, I am determined and driven. And I do care. Very much.

So here is my New Year's resolution: I am hence forth banned from using a defence against failure that pretty much guarantees I will not succeed. After all in the words of Henry Ford: 'If you think that you can or you think that you can't, you are usually right.'

So I will enter events aiming to pull out a peak performance and to compete for placings every time. I will stop feeling apologetic if I mess up and start feeling bloody annoyed instead. I will never again express any doubts about my rightful place as Amber's rider and our rightful place at ODEs. After all with a jump as effortlessly joyful as hers, there is nowhere better for us to be.

Oh and I guess I'd better learn to plait

Stop pre-empting judgements by being self-judgemental and putting yourself down. It may feel like humility, but it really isn't helpful. If you care, then say so. If you want to do well, then set yourself up for success. If you are ambitious, own that, and don't be afraid to set challenging goals and work towards them. It's fine to let yourself be vulnerable. These self-protective masks are destructive because:

- You start believing you truly don't belong
- You feel defensive even though no-one is attacking you
- You fail to prepare for success by expecting to be a bit rubbish
- Failure can therefore become self-fulfilling.

Habit

Another reason people don't drop Parrot-Speak is because it has simply become a habit. They get so used to having a critical internal dialogue that they don't question it, don't recognize that the dialogue is optional, and therefore they never consider disengaging from it or re-writing the script. This can be particularly the case if people identify trauma in childhood as the root of their internalized self-criticism. They find it hard to believe that they can simply set that parental baggage down and say 'I'm not a child anymore. I don't need to listen to this anymore.'

I'm a therapist and, of course, some people may need to go into therapy in order to explore and address long standing roots to current distress. But many actually don't need to do that. Or even if they do, they can still disengage from critical parental voices anytime they choose.

A Form of Reassurance Seeking

If people vocalise how rubbish they feel about their riding, they often hope that others will boost their confidence by telling them that they are doing much better than they think they are. Yes they might. That reassurance may make them feel slightly better for a short while, but external validation is nowhere near as effective or powerful as internal confidence.

In addition, giving the Parrot's squawking criticism airtime strengthens its voice, which you definitely don't want. By all means be honest about your feelings, but there is a difference between saying 'I can lack confidence jumping, so can we start small and build up', versus saying 'I am a total wimp when it comes to jumping. I am terrified and I'll probably cry. Frankly I'm a lost cause.' The former is useful communication. The latter is destructive Parrot-Speak.

Problem Solving

Some people have a belief that if they think of every possible eventuality that might go wrong, then they can make sure those things don't happen. But this does not work. Preparing well is not the same as worrying. You can anticipate certain challenges, and plan for them, but you can't deal with something that has not yet happened.

A Reverse Sort of Arrogance

I certainly don't mean to offend anyone by suggesting their Parrot's insistence that they are an embarrassing waste of space if they ever have a wobble, is actually a form of arrogance. But this is certainly something that I have experienced myself, and is something clients bring to me. So I'll put it out there: It takes humility to be bad at something. It takes humility to publicly struggle with something. It takes humility to be the person who needs the most help in a lesson or who comes last in a race. But every lesson and every race will have someone who struggles a bit more, or someone who comes last. Why should that never be you?

Why is it ok for others to struggle, and for you to graciously support them, but not ok for you to struggle and for others to offer their support to you? Why is it ok for you to cheer on the person coming in last at a race, but not for you to be the last runner being cheered home. It is a form of arrogance to believe that struggling or being last is humiliating for you, but fine for anyone else. What makes you so special?

During the early days of triathlon racing I was having a bit of a whinge about being a Back-Of-The-Packer to my husband. I had been doing the Beaver Tri which had the run set out over 4 laps. I was so far behind that as I came towards the start/finish line at the end of lap 3, everyone assumed I was finishing and a great cheer went up. Which sputtered into embarrassed silence as I ignored the left turn down the finishing chute and instead went straight on to start another lap.

My husband said he had huge admiration for people who went out with no chance of getting in the top half. The ones running purely for the joy of setting personally meaningful goals and achieving them. He wasn't sure his ego would allow him to do a race where he was in the bottom 10%, the way I did over and over again. And it occurred to me that the only reason there are so many well attended races is because of those who are willing to be 'below average'. If no-one was willing to be below average, all races or events would have about 6 people in them, all aiming for the podium.

It made me think more about what I viewed as an achievement. I had long since stopped trying to be competitive. I went as fast as I could, and took the training seriously, but still had the tendency to see my achievements as slightly inadequate, and to feel embarrassed by my finishing times. I needed to recognise the huge value in the simple willingness to set personally challenging goals, and to keep exploring and expanding my own perceived limits. I also needed to recognise the distinct lack of arrogance or ego in being willing to be last. I decided to celebrate flying the flag of mediocrity, thinking that maybe my willingness to take part, even though I was slow, might encourage others to give it a go too. I felt and still feel that really would be an achievement.

Similarly, I encourage riders to think about the fact that they too can model the value in gracious acceptance of help, willingness to be vulnerable, willingness to keep it real, and to show the effort and the struggles they go through, as well as the instagrammable moments. I love a good pic as much as the rest of us. But I am truly inspired by those who share the disasters as well as the triumphs. The Parrot would have you believe that struggling is humiliating. The Parrot is wrong.

Comparisonitis

It is hard not to compare ourselves to others. However, it is even harder not to compare ourselves to former versions of ourselves. There are many reasons why a person may no longer be able to do things they used to find easy. Sometimes the change is temporary, sometimes it is long term or permanent. Many women find that they lose their confidence, and are less willing to take risks, after having children. Many older people recognize that they don't bounce like they used to, and scale back their ambitions. Many riders who have had or witnessed accidents feel more vulnerable, and less willing to jump the way they once did.

I am aware myself that when I fall off it usually leaves me with some sort of physical issue. Whereas when I was younger, falls generally had little physical impact on me. I have also become aware that injuries take longer to heal than they did when I was younger.

These changes may be magnified for anyone who has developed an illness or disability that affects their reaction times, their balance, their focus, or their recovery rates.

Some of these issues can be temporary, and others can be noticed without confidence being affected. I am conscious of being older, more injury prone, and taking longer to heal, but as yet those insights have not slowed me down. However, I have had to start right back at the beginning, more than once, to be able to move forward. Parrot can be very sabotaging in such situations, telling riders that they 'should' be further on than they are, that it is 'embarrassing' to be at a level so far below where they used to be, and so on.

Some changes that affect skill are, however, long term or permanent. In these difficult situations it is important to come to terms with that, to find ways to celebrate other achievements, and to discover new goals that inspire you. Comparisons with old versions of yourself are self-limiting, and dwelling on how you used to perform or feel is pointless and destructive. This mindset will also stop you moving forward. Progress is only possible by going back as far as you need to, to ride safely and skillfully. And by adjusting goals so they reflect new realities. Refusal to do this leaves you stuck in a frustrating limbo.

An inspirational example of the futility of comparing yourself now to your past performances, comes from the Irish eventing star, Jonty Evans, who sustained a serious brain injury after a fall from his horse, Art, at the 2018 Tattersalls International Horse Trials in Ireland.

His eventing Facebook page provides wonderful examples of resilience and the value of a positive mindset. He is very open about how hard it is not to be able to ride the way he used to, but he refuses to give up and he accepts his current limitations. In doing so, he is not relinquishing ambition – far from it – but is simply acknowledging where he is right now, and taking the steps needed to make progress from there. He still has hopes and dreams, he still works incredibly hard on those. And he is still setting and achieving impressive and ambitious goals. None of that would be possible if he were not willing to let go of comparisons, and accept that he is where he is, and can only move forward from that place, even if he would prefer to be starting from somewhere else.

In June 2022, he wrote: "Art was his usual fab self [at British Dressage]. He scored 65% and 66% in the mediums. While they are not scores to shout about yet, they were a big improvement on last time we were out. Comparing my performance to where I was pre-accident is not good. A couple of people have pointed that out. Comparing myself and Art to how we were when we were out a few weeks ago is far more useful and isn't that the way everyone does it? Art did win both classes! So I suppose that's a positive!"

He is also producing a young horse which has helped him avoid comparing his riding now to his pre-accident level, writing: "Trying to come to terms with where my riding is now is actually helped a LOT by producing my young horse because I'm not comparing myself all the time to where I was!! Many people including my mum and sister (who knows better than most how self-critical I am) have told me to give myself a pat on the back for producing him so far!!"

As well he should.

I gave up ultra-running some years ago due to chronic injuries. I recently decided to try and get going again because one particular, quirky event appeals to me. I am exploring whether I can regain any running consistency, or whether I will break down again. I have no idea but am prepared to start slow and see where I get to.

I recently did my first 5k Parkrun for many years. 5k used to feel like a distance hardly worth getting out of bed for. But is now a genuinely huge challenge. I made my peace with that, but felt slightly awkward hanging right back at the start, and avoiding eye contact with people who knew me in the 'old days'.

However, I was spotted and a chap came over. 'Hey not seen you for ages. Are you running?' he asked. I said that I was planning to run but may just do 2 of the 3 laps as I had not run for a long time.

He commented: 'wow last time I bumped into you out running you were training for a triple marathon. How times change.'

'Tell me about it' I said ruefully. 'But I've got to start somewhere.'

He then explained he was in the same situation – age and injury having stopped him from running. He was also just giving it a go, and was unlikely to make the full

5k. This was a useful reminder that having to re-set and start small, is *normal*. The only question is: are you willing to accept where you are and make progress from there? Or are you going to give up, because you can't face taking 2 or 20 and 200 steps back? 5k is an ambitious challenge for me now. For others, a 5 minute walk/run might be a genuine achievement. And for yet others, it's walking 5 steps unaided across a hospital ward. It is all relative, and wherever you are is where you are. From there, where do you want to go?

I did the run and genuinely felt proud that I made it round all 3 laps. I am excited about where I might go next. As ever, indulging Parrot is a choice. I chose to smile, hold my head up high and give it my best shot. I know that I can never get back to where I was a decade ago. Frankly, who can? But I can still set and achieve personally meaningful goals, even if they are a long way off where I used to be. The Parrot would say where I am now is hopeless and embarrassing. Once again, the Parrot is wrong.

Hurray my Parrot has been Shot. Now What?

Let's just say you have managed to identify and disarm Parrot-speak. You are no longer listening. You have filled your mind with positivity and dropped unhelpful stories. You are mentally focused, well prepared and connected to your skills. You have clear goals that are authentic and meaningful to you. You are confident and the Chimp is safely in his cage. Problem solved? Well no, not always, because there is one final critter in the mental menagerie who gets in the way. It's time to get to know the Mouse.

CHAPTER 8

The Doubting Mouse

Picture the scene. You are in a jumping lesson, jumping round a 70cm course confidently. You have a lovely, rhythmic canter, you are looking well ahead and the fences all seem to magically appear in front of you in exactly the right place. Your horse lands and turns fluidly and is always on the right leg. You feel as though you have acres of space and plenty of time. The round flows beautifully.

Then all the jumps get raised a hole or 2. And that inviting, flowing 70 course now looks mountainous. You express your misgivings to your instructor who breezily tells you that the horse won't even notice a 5-10cm increase in height. You set off again, but that confidence has been replaced by doubt and uncertainty. The first fence looks huge, you can't see the stride, and you half-halt, trying to find one, while staring at the fence. You bury your horse into the base of the jump and he clambers over it, making you lose balance. The canter is flat, the rhythm has gone and he breaks to trot on the turn. You kick into canter again and awkwardly jump the 2nd, then have 5 strides instead of 4 down to the related distance at 3. 4 looks big again so you kick on, but you are staring at the fence instead of the line, so when the horse lands he has no idea where he is going next. He travels straight for a few strides and misses the turn back to 5. 'Stop, stop!' shouts your instructor. You know it was a mess of a round.

What on earth was that all about? You have not suddenly forgotten how to ride. And horses really don't notice a 5-10cm difference. What is happening?

Essentially you have stopped riding from feel and started trying too hard. Doubt has crept in and, in response, your thinking brain has tried to take over. You lose trust in your innate skills. These qualms are then transferred to your body in the form of tension, tightness, rigidity and awkwardness. You lose timing and feel. You stop seeing the course clearly, instead either fixating on things like the fences, fillers or water trays, and losing sight of the lines and the overall space. You stop riding a flowing sequence, linking lines naturally, which leads you to automatically use the space well. Instead, you start seeing the course as a series of individual jumps, and the space shrinks around you. Fluidity vanishes, replaced with effortful awkwardness.

We ride best when our mind is quiet, focused and aware. Awareness is not the same as thinking. With quiet, focused awareness we don't have to think. We already *know.*

The Power of Awareness

With awareness, we know where the lines go. We don't land then look for the next fence.

With awareness, we feel what canter we need, and we maintain that feel through continuous automatic adjustments, not through noticing changes and then over-correcting via mental instruction.

Almost all of us have, from time to time, experienced 'breakthrough' rides where it feels effortless and easy, and we ride far above our usual level. These are characterized by awareness, not by thinking. It does not happen through trying harder. Rather it is a non-thinking, spontaneous state, when everything flows. These rides show us that we have more ability locked inside than we can normally access. That, although work and effort matter, to really ride at our best we need to stop consciously trying. A great ride should not feel like hard work.

Riding through feel and awareness can only happen when the mind is quiet. When we feel what is happening underneath us and within our own bodies. We make endless tiny adjustments to maintain rhythm, position and balance. We are naturally coordinated, fluid and supple. We are fully aware of our surroundings. We are in our bodies and not up in our heads, overthinking. Time feels suspended; external distractions silenced. Just you, your horse and the test or course. The gymnast, Jessica Gadirova, described this beautifully in an interview after a stunning floor routine. She said it was 'just me and the floor' and described her mind as quiet, calm and focused. During the routine, she was able to – in her words – 'just flow.'

In tennis matches, momentum shifts one way or another. Levels rise and fall on both sides of the net throughout the match. Players look effortlessly balanced, always in the right place, always over the ball in an athletic stance, striking sweetly, finding the lines, executing featherlight drop shots with exquisite feel. Or they look flat-footed, off balance, missing lines, sending easy smashes into the net and peppering the court with mis-hits. How often do we see a wonderful reflexive volley at the net? And how many times do we see a defensive lob go up and there is just too much time to think about it, as the ball hangs in the air for an age, and the player fluffs it?

The players aren't gaining and losing skills during the match. They are just moving in and out of playing in 'The Zone' with awareness and feel, versus overthinking, getting tight and trying too hard. With those lightning quick exchanges at the net, there is often no room for the Mouse to butt in. With the ball in the air for ages, there is far too much time, and suddenly instructions like 'don't mess this up' or 'focus' appear. Ironically, telling yourself to 'pay attention' is distracting.

Timothy Gallwey, author of 'The Inner Game' series of sport coaching books, talks of Player 1 and Player 2 in all sports.

Player 1 is the voice of self-instruction, muttering things like 'where's the stride', 'that's too big' 'we need more speed', 'those turns are too tight' and 'this arena is tiny.'

Player 2 is your natural, innate balance, timing, feel and skill. Spoiler alert: Player 2 is a much better rider when Player 1 shuts up.

Player 1 takes up a number of roles, some of which overlap with the Parrot. But the Parrot is a fairly mindless process of self-criticism and bullying, whereas the Mouse does try to help. He's just often counter-productive.

Mouse can act like an instructor: shoulders back, heels down, head up, stop bouncing, hands still and so forth. Mouse may try to hijack PMA statements by turning them into a set of instructions. This is not helpful. PMA Statements are used to create the right *feel* and should help you achieve a quiet, focused, positive, mindset. They are not an opportunity to over-think.

Mouse can draw your attention to unhelpful things: that fence is huge, that turn is tight, that line is awkward, that filler is spooky. Mouse is trying to help, but you do not need this input and it's very off putting. When walking a course, Awareness decides 'this is how I need to ride that line', using imagery and visualization.

Just seeing what you will need to do. Whereas Mouse might say 'you need to be careful here. It's an awkward line. Don't let him run out. This is very tricky.' It is a subtle difference: Awareness sees the line and fully focuses on it. Awareness knows what you need to do to prevent a run out to the left or the right. Or that you need to line up with the related distance behind. Whereas Mouse doubts your ability to ride the line, or prevent a run out, and makes you doubt too.

Mouse can be self-conscious: 'everyone is watching,' and can react by trying to hide and be invisible or by trying to impress everyone. Either way, the focus shifts to other people when it needs to be on you, your horse, and the task or the course. We need to cultivate a goal-oriented focus, not an internal ego-driven self-conscious focus, such as a sudden image of what you feel you look like to others, or what other people think.

Self-consciousness is a significant problem for some people. Skills they can access readily when they are alone, or being watched by people they feel comfortable around, evaporate instantly if they are being watched by a ride judge, an examiner, an Olympian sharing the same schooling facility, their team mates or a parent.

The problem with self-consciousness is that it leads to a shift from a task-oriented focus to an internal, viewer-oriented one. This is very commonly seen in people who struggle with public speaking. To speak well we need to concentrate on what we are saying. Not on what we look like or how our voice sounds. As soon as we shift attention inwards to ourselves, and wonder about how other people are seeing us, images of ourselves looking red or stuttering come to mind. This interrupts our ability to focus on what we are doing or saying. We hear our own voice and it sounds weak or hesitant. This is enormously distracting and anxiety provoking, and we lose access to our skills.

In this situation, you have stopped focusing on the talk or task itself, and Mouse has taken over, presenting you with ideas about how you are coming across, how you sound, how you look, how you are riding, how bouncy your hands are or whatever. None of which is helpful at all.

The difference between an inward, self-conscious, and an outward, task-oriented focus of attention is huge. It involves such a simple shift in perspective but the experiences transform like night and day. When you are externally focused you are more single minded, more aware, more absorbed or immersed, more mindful, more creative, and more solution orientated. When your attention shifts internally, you are self-conscious and distracted from the task by thoughts about how you look or by judgements. You lose focus and clarity. Awareness is diluted. You may feel anxious, exposed, or embarrassed, or you may try to impress and enjoy an opportunity to show off. Either way, your mind is no longer task or goal focused but is rooted in what others are seeing, how you are looking and how you are doing. As soon as you start to evaluate your performance *while still performing*, then you lose clarity and focus.

KEY CONCEPT:
Focus on the task, not on how you might look and sound to others.

It is much more effective if you are able to prevent the focus of your attention from shifting to other people, instead focusing on what you are doing, the feel of what you want and the task at hand. You may need to rehearse this via visualization at first. You can practice this with some helpful buddies, deliberately shifting your attention between focusing on them and what they can see or might be thinking, versus focusing on the horse and the task at hand. Even if the buddies don't trigger self-consciousness, as you feel comfortable with them, it is useful to be able to experience the difference between riding with an outward versus an internal focus of attention. This helps you become skilled at shifting back to the task when you have found yourself getting distracted by people watching you, or by feelings of self-consciousness.

When people are fully focused and present, they can become so absorbed by what they are doing that they are unaware of their surroundings, other people, sensations like cold, whether it is raining and even the passage of time. The Canadian show jumper, Ian Millar, describes barn time as being outside of 'real time' saying hours can fly by. It takes the time it takes, and he stays calmly, patiently focused, present and aware until he has achieved what he set out to achieve at the start of the session.

Cultivating Flow

We ride best when we are in a state of 'flow' or in 'The Zone'. This is where our minds are calm and quiet and we are alert, aware, mindful and determined. The Mouse and Parrot are silenced, while the Chimp is on side, firing us up, and improving our reflexes, concentration and drive.

We can't force 'flow' or The Zone. All we can do is create the conditions for flow and allow it. The best way to do that is to get out of our own way and let it happen.

Thinking Trust Not Try, focusing on feel and awareness and staying present are all helpful.

Mouse represents the opposite of flow. Flow states cannot be forced by trying. Mouse tries too hard. Flow is characterised by an absence of thought. Mouse is a never-shutting-up instructor constantly telling you what you need to do.

Mouse sometimes pretends to be the aware and innately skilful Player 2 by giving instructions like STOP TRYING SO HARD AND JUST FEEL. Do not be fooled. If you are telling yourself you need to be in Player 2 mode then you are definitely not. Player 2 is not thinking about being Player 2. Player 2 just is.

We can cultivate flow in a number of ways.

- Have a clear goal in mind. Flow arises when we are clear about what we want and know exactly what 'success' feels like. 'Success' is, of course, defined entirely by you. Success might mean a wonderful ambling ride in nature, at one with the horse and the environment. You can experience flow just reading a book, when you fall into the story, becoming fully immersed in the world within the book.

- Have personally meaningful goals. For flow states to arise we need to value the goal or task and feel deeply satisfied by it.

- In goals related to improvements, we are more likely to experience flow when we are near the edge – but not beyond – our current ability. If the task is too easy we may fall into auto-pilot. If it is much too hard we are likely to get anxious. If it is in the Learning Zone, just beyond the edge of our ability, then we are likely to be making mistakes. This Zone is fantastic for improving. However, the sweet spot for flow is at the upper limit of our ability, when 'working the edge'. These are the situation most likely to lead to those wonderful performance breakthroughs.

- We are willing to set time aside and stay focused and single minded as we work towards our goal. As Ian Millar said 'the task is done when it is done', and 'barn time' is outside of normal time.
- We maintain concentration for a period of time. We do not get distracted by shifting to judgements, by switching to instructor mode, or by setting up instagrammable shots while we try to achieve our goals. If someone is taking pictures, great. I love a good picture too. But, ideally, you would not be aware of the photographer. If you are constantly looking for where she is and thinking 'hope she is taking this one' as you head for a fence, you will interrupt flow.

Neuro-science studies show that flow states are very real, associated with deep concentration, calmness and focus, as well as pleasure, satisfaction and happiness. If we can silence the Mouse and spend more time in flow, we will not only enhance our riding, but also our lives. However, flow states are fragile and easily disrupted. It is important that you set the conditions for flow as often as possible and that you protect and nurture emerging states of flow.

> **KEY CONCEPT:**
> **Achieving flow is the holy grail for riders. Set the conditions for flow, then protect and nurture it.**

Trust Don't Try

The route to better riding is silencing the Mouse and riding from timing and feel.

You may be familiar with the stages of learning from unconscious incompetence, (you don't know that you are doing something badly), to conscious incompetence, (you have become aware of what you can't yet do well), conscious competence, (you can do something but have to really focus hard on it and – finally – unconscious competence. Also known as Player 2, Mouse free riding.

Less familiar is the idea that unconscious competence is not just a stage you attain after a certain amount of time, but a mindset you can actively cultivate at any stage of learning. On the other hand, you can ride for 50 years and still have Player 1 (conscious competence) as the dominant mind-state in which you ride.

Unconscious competence is a state of awareness, and you can develop awareness from your earliest lessons. You can sit on a horse and think 'pull back to stop, kick to go, pull rein right to turn that way, pull rein left to turn the other way.' And then spend your whole first lesson inside your head trying to remember what to do.

Or you can let the instructor control the horse and just feel what happens. Feel your legs move side to side as his barrel moves. Feel your hips rise and fall as his back lifts and dips. When you come to use the rein, you can feel what happens if you move it this way or that. We really aren't taught like that very often. But it makes a huge difference to how comfortable and familiar we can quickly feel, and how rapidly unconscious competence develops.

Kids who initially learn to ride by being plonked on the back of a small pony, aged 3, and led in from the field bareback, have far better balance and feel, than those at 6, carefully given a load of instructions to try and remember.

Think about the process of learning to walk. No one teaches a child to walk. They do it by trial and error. By feel. And they pick the skills up effortlessly, then rapidly gain more skills, once they have mastered those first stumbling steps. Before you know it, they are running and climbing and jumping. All without any instruction whatsoever.

Children learn to walk through feedback loops. If they take a step and stumble there is no immediate outcry from Parrot and Mouse. No Parrot saying 'what an idiot, you'll never be able to do this.' No Mouse insisting 'pay attention, shift weight forward, widen your stance, careful!' There is just a natural adjustment based on the feedback loop. If a toddler used self-instruction, Player 1 would be so busy telling them how to walk that they would lose touch with the feel of it. And end up on their bum again.

Children don't break down a physical challenge into separate sequences. They absorb the task as a whole. And yet verbal instruction tends to be sequential: this, then this, then this. Riding involves your whole body doing many different things at once. It is impossible to ride well through self-instruction. You need to *feel* what to do.

A great example of the debilitating effect of Mouse was recognised over 100 years ago in this famous 19th Century poem:

> A centipede was happy – quite!
> Until a toad in fun
> Said, "Pray, which leg moves after which?"
> This raised her doubts to such a pitch,
> She fell exhausted in the ditch
> Not knowing how to run.

KEY CONCEPT:
When we start doubting, we lose touch with our skills and they fall apart.

It is hard to banish doubt when we have too much time to think. Consider serving at Championship point or a trying to score a match winning (or losing) penalty at a major football tournament. However skilled people are, they need to manage those doubts, to access their skills, and take a decent penalty, or serve a good first serve.

England's football tournament history is littered with top level professionals who scuff or sky the ball on penalties – leading papers to scream 'WHY DON'T THEY PRACTICE PENALTIES.' Of course they practice penalties! It is not a skill problem, it's a Mouse one. Solved not by more practice or trying harder, but by developing a mindset in which you can stay present, in the moment, locked into the feel you need. Where you switch off your brain and let your body do what it has done a thousand times, and can do easily.

It is fascinating looking at the penalty conversion rate under different situations. The task is exactly the same every time: A ball 12 yards from the goal. One player trying to kick the ball into the net, and another player trying to keep it out. And yet the conversion rate varies dramatically depending on the mental state of the players.

In the Premier League, the penalty conversion rate is over 83%. Goals matter in any game, so any penalty involves some pressure, but this level of pressure is manageable, and a very high proportion of penalties are successfully taken.

However, in a penalty shoot-out situation, the pressure becomes immeasurably higher. There have been over 200 penalty shoot-outs in World Cup history. The conversion rate for the first one or two is 75%. A lot lower than in the Premier League but still quite high. By penalty 4 it has dropped to 64%. Then there is another big drop when it comes to sudden death, from penalty 5 onwards, with a conversion rate of only 50%.

These statistics remain very similar even if a team mixes up the penalty taking order so their best penalty takers come on for sudden death penalties. Sancho, Saka, Rashford, Gascoigne, Trezeguet, Baggio, Beckham and Kane – all fantastic strikers and midfield players, have missed penalties during knock-out phases of major tournaments.

Superstition is also Mouse: 'We always lose to Germany', 'we always lose on penalties', etc. These beliefs introduce doubt, then the Mouse takes over and the superstition becomes a self-fulfilling prophecy. It is common for a rider who normally goes clear cross-country, but has show-jumping faults, to react to a clear round of show-jumping by immediately thinking 'I'm bound to have cross-country penalties now.' By thinking like that, they make that outcome more likely.

We can't banish Mouse. But we can be aware that doubt leads to overtrying and that, in turn, causes us to lose access to our skills. Cultivating the ability to stay focused, present, and in your body rather than your mind, takes hours, weeks, months or years of patient practice. Nonetheless, there are many examples of sportsmen and women who have learned to manage their Mouse, and to play with more focus and feel when the pressure mounts.

And of course, those who never did. For example, Jimmy White, who made it to 6 snooker world championship finals and never won. Including in 1994 when he just needed an easy black to take the Championship. He got nowhere near it.

KEY CONCEPT:
Doubt and superstition make feared outcomes far more likely

Indecision

The Mouse also represents indecision: the horrible feeling of simply not knowing what to do, and therefore endlessly talking yourself out of doing anything at all. Black flagged jumps used to really throw me, as they introduced doubt. The question was no longer 'how will I jump this' but 'WILL I jump this?' Regardless of what a fence was actually like, if it was black flagged I, (Mouse), always decided it looked dodgy and started weighing up time faults versus the risk of 20 penalties.

Then one day I was dithering over a fence that I have done before, that is not normally black flagged, and the same 'will I/won't I' debate started up. I realised the fence was not the problem. The problems were DOUBT and INDECISION. I decided there and then that I was going the direct route, no matter what, for every fence, at every event. I simply don't even allow myself to ask the question anymore, and that has been very helpful in keeping the Mouse silent.

Doubt can also be very problematic when it comes to warm-ups. Some readers may be thinking, 'for heaven's sake if you can't warm-up confidently you are definitely not ready to compete.' Other readers will be thinking 'I thought it was just me!' Warming up is actually a significant problem for some riders. And Mouse is the reason why.

In a competition, the fences are arranged in a specific and fixed order. The only decisions to be made are how to ride the course. Plus, once you enter the ring the FIGHT element of Chimp wakes up, and nerves often evaporate. However, in the warm-up, you have Chimp saying 'bad idea, best avoided,' and you have Mouse querying every suggestion you come up with. While Parrot tells you what an idiot you are because you can't even warm your horse up properly.

I remember having this issue at Chatsworth for the arena eventing. There was an ambulance hold before I even got into the warm-up area, following a rider fall. The atmosphere was intense and my horse was a bit unsettled as I walked her round in small circles, waiting to go in. I could also see the ambulance and the injured rider. That increased Chimp's reluctance and ridiculous phrases like 'maybe it's a sign to pull out' came into my mind. I labelled those thoughts 'Chimp-Speak' and ignored them, but they left an emotional residue.

When I finally went in, the warm-up arena was more crowded than usual, as more and more riders had turned up for their rounds. There was no system for staggering the number of people allowed in, so it was very busy. The event was on grass and it was the first time I had jumped that horse on grass. And it was wet. It was also quite a narrow space, with railings on one side and a river on the other. There was a large tree with low branches at one end. My awareness was limited as I was getting hyper-focused on the jumps. As I turned to my first cross-pole I rode into an overhanging branch, smacking myself in the face with a bunch of wet leaves.

Parrot launched into a frenzy of 'how embarrassing, you are a joke.' Again, I ignored that and just cantered round slowly, paying a bit more attention to the tree. I thought about jumping an upright, but my risk perception was now distorted (thanks, Chimp) so I chickened out first time round. Then I broke to trot as I turned to it, as I was not riding forward enough. Chickened out again. Then there were too many people around and I did not feel I had enough space. Then, then, then.....

Before I knew it, my number was being called and I went in to jump a big, technical course after warming up over a single cross-pole from trot. After that I recognized I needed to address indecision in warm-ups.

Reduce Indecision by Having a Plan

To start with, I decided to treat the warm-up as part of the round. Totally non-negotiable. I told myself that if I can't prepare her properly, then it's not fair to jump her, so get a grip and get on with it, or withdraw.

I now give my pre-competition routines as much priority as the round itself, to the extent that I mentally commentate on my warm-up. 'And Krissie is just moving through the gears now, establishing control, making sure all the buttons work... Lottie looks nicely relaxed.... And now she is moving to the jumping phase, with a confidence giving cross-pole to begin with' sort of thing. Sounds mad but it helps to trick my brain and fire up my Chimp. This also reminds me of the purpose of each part of the process, as the 'commentator' is explaining it. This helps me give it more importance, which increases my focus, keeps the Chimp in his cage, and the Mouse quiet.

I also have a very clear plan, developed with my instructor, and practiced. This helps soothe Mouse as I am not trying to decide what to do. I already know what I am going to do. If things are not going to plan, and I need to adjust, then I channel my instructor. I literally picture her in the middle, by the jumps, as she talks me through what I need to do.

Of course, I don't know exactly what she might say I should do. But that is not really relevant. In this exercise I simply picture her and imagine the advice she offers. I then do what I am told which means I don't avoid. Therefore I achieve a warm-up with some logic behind it, regardless of whether or not what 'she' tells me to do in my own head bears any relation to what she would actually say if she were there.

This exercise differs from Mouse-As-Instructor because vividly imagining someone knowledgeable often leads to insights or recommendations arising that feel outside my own head. I then simply need to obey. This feels very different to the stream of contradictory advice Mouse gives me.

2-chair work is a technique in psychotherapy which makes use of this phenomenon: In 2-chair work the person role plays someone from their past, or a younger version of themselves. They process the world very differently, when acting as someone else, and thus, perceive their situation in new, and often unexpected ways.

The most bizarre personal experience of this I have had, was when driving our new car. I realized, when I stopped for fuel, that I did not have the petrol cap key on my key ring. I asked the garage to break it off, so I could re-fuel, and carried on my journey with a temporary plastic cap. I relayed this mishap in an imaginary conversation with my husband. Inside my own head, he instantly replied: 'but Krissie there isn't a separate petrol cap key. It's just the ignition key.' My husband would never make a mistake like that – and so he corrected MY mistake inside my own mind.

Pre-Competition Routines

It is also very useful to have a specific and well-rehearsed routine every time you compete. Or serve, or take penalties. This might involve the warm-up, but can also include other forms of preparation, such as visualization, PMA statements, particular music tracks, and exercises like power posing, muscle activation exercises or a stretch routine. The aim is to create the conditions for peak performance. It has nothing to do with actually practicing skills. It is about entering the right mindset to access those skills. The goal is to think less and achieve flow: calm, focused, alert, aware. Physically and psychologically ready for the challenge.

One of my clients, Ellie, uses music very effectively, as part of her pre-competition routines. She chose the song 'Powerful', by Major Lazer, for both jumping phases. She goes into the lorry and plays the song with eyes closed, while visualising the round. She has always walked the course by then, and knows it inside out. The song starts slowly and Ellie imagines warming up, with everything unfolding absolutely perfectly. When the song first hits the chorus, and goes up-tempo, Ellie imagines a rein-back to canter and the pony jumps forward, fully off the leg and feeling punchy. The chorus goes: 'I can feel it, there's an energy, when you hold me, when you touch me, it's so powerful', then repeats. As she listens, she pictures jumping each fence during the chorus, rewinding where needed to make sure she has jumped every fence on the course in imagination, with those lyrics, and that tempo running through her mind. She finds this psyches her up.

She explains, 'my first BE double-clear was after doing this for the first time, and it's now something I always do. I channel the energy from the song, and it feels like Lola and I are totally fired up, and really focused. It is just so helpful.'

Paralysis By Analysis

Having a plan is important, but sometimes external events mean that you have to rapidly re-think and adjust. In that situation, Mouse can find fault with any options you come up with, leaving you in a state of indecision about what to do.

Mouse's indecision invites Parrot and Chimp to the party, and they all get involved, leaving the hapless rider stressed, unsure, unfocused, anxious and upset. Not an easy way to ride.

This became very clear to me recently when I went to an eventer trial. I wanted to go double-clear and be in with a chance of a win. I had jumped clear several times at full ODEs, always to be let down by the dressage test.

A jumping only event seemed perfect for us. My horse was usually bang on the optimum time, so placing high, or even winning, seemed perfectly possible. I was fired up and ready to attack the course. Then I walked it and saw that a jump had been placed in the middle of the water towards the end of the course. Not a tiny log either, but a solid, 3 log stack. I had never jumped that horse in water before, and felt it was bad training to ask that of her, without preparing her properly for the question.

I started wondering about treating the round like a training round and missing out that fence. From my initial perspective of riding to win, I had 'failed' before I even started, as I was obviously going to be eliminated. I struggled to get positive and fired up for an unexpected training round. Mouse would not commit to that plan, but kept saying 'well maybe I should at least give it a try.' But then when I tried to psych myself up to jump it, Mouse argued against that too, saying 'but it's bad training.'

I did not have time to get my head around the change of plan and I was annoyed at what I considered a totally inappropriate question for the level. The fence had been marked with a yellow (novice) sticker when all the others were orange (90cm). I had gone to ask show officials whether it was actually in the course and was (I felt) patronized with a 'yes, is there a problem love' reply. Hence, I was warming up feeling a mixture of embarrassed, angry, and tearful. I was in a state of total indecision. I thought that asking my horse to jump that fence was bad training, but I was also questioning whether I was falling under the spell of the Chimp, and just needed to attack the course. Whether I was letting nerves talk me out of it. I was upset and had little time, so I could not get a plan straight in my mind. It was like washing up with a dirty dish-cloth. An upset, Chimp-filled, Parrot-filled, Mouse driven brain was struggling to identify the wise-mind option.

Looking back, I think treating it like a training round would have been the right choice. If I had had more time, I would have found a way to get focused and motivated for that. I also feel that attacking the course was a reasonable option too. I should have made a decision, one way or another, then refused to pay any attention to any further internal debate. Either of the 2 options was better than unsure dithering.

However, I went in still wracked with indecision and frustration. A state of mind not improved by the start-bell not going. I cantered round while my frustration about what I was now thinking of as 'a bloody shambles of an event' was increasingly amplified. I eventually asked and was told the bell had already gone. I spun to gallop to the first fence, fearing elimination. Then the bell went. I thought I was eliminated so pulled her out, only for people to shout 'that's the bell' at me. Cue a 2nd spin and gallop to the fence, which was not necessary as

I could have just had time faults. But I was not thinking straight.

I rode a shocking show-jumping round, in which my horse saved me repeatedly, but we were both thoroughly rattled by the time we headed out cross-country which followed on immediately from the show-jumping phase. I had 2 refusals at the first 2 cross-country fences, before dropping to smaller fences, which had become the only ones that looked jumpable to my wildly untogether brain.

I had gone out onto the course in a state of indecision and frustration. As a result I was eliminated way before reaching the only fence I was concerned about.

To put being eliminated into context, I did 9 other events that season, and went clear cross-country in all but 1 of them. The only cross-country fault I had was a glance off the 2nd element of a related distance that I rode a terrible line to. She is a very genuine cross-country horse. But trying to ride her around a course when I was indecisive, lacking in focus, and negative highlighted the importance of mental attitude, even on a genuine, bold horse.

Just to be clear, I am not complaining about the event. The problems I had were entirely down to me. It is up to course builders what courses they build, and up to riders to decide on their plan of attack. Or strategic retreat. The event did not frustrate and upset me. I allowed myself to become upset and frustrated by elements of the event that did not meet my (unrealistic) expectations. Good performances depend on the ability to stay calm and focused, and to not let yourself get annoyed or distracted. I have done plenty of events where things have gone pear-shaped. I have been sent the wrong direction to find the cross-country or dressage, broken down on the way there, forgotten important kit, learned the wrong test, been held on course or been told it's a bell when actually it was a horn. I've had dogs running loose and a helicopter taking off right beside the cross-country warm-up. Events are unpredictable. It is up to the competitor to deal with issues as they arise, calmly and effectively, and then get on with it.

This relates directly to the Dilts framework discussed in Chapter 1. I was operating at the superficial levels of 1 and 2: Environment and Behaviour. I was telling myself a 'problem' or 'not fair' or 'chaotic event' story, and blaming my problems on those external factors. Whereas, in fact, I was entirely responsible for how I rode, and all the problems I had out on course came from bad riding.

I completely failed to take personal responsibility and therefore made a total mess of it. I had the option of firing myself up and attacking the course. The jump in water was on the way home and by then she could well have been full of confidence and just nailed it. I could have won. Alternatively, I could have calmly decided to treat it as a training round, and run through the water past the jump, but done everything else with full commitment. Either option would have been fine. Instead, I dithered and fretted and let external conditions affect me. Then gave myself and my horse a terrible ride. But it was a very powerful lesson in the importance of a) mental attitude, b) taking responsibility for how I ride rather than blaming external events and c) the need to override Mouse's indecision. To simply make a decision and then follow through.

Staying Present

All the exercises discussed earlier for maintaining present moment awareness, are also helpful in silencing the Mouse. Re-visit those chapters. Visualizations are as important here as everywhere else. Mentally run through every element of your competition, including warm-ups, test moves, lines and the ways in which you intend to ride. Come up with PMA statements that centre on getting you into the right head-space. PMA statements are not an invitation to over-think. They are phrases that trigger a feeling or a mental attitude that allows you to ride effectively.

'Focus and fire', for example, acts as shorthand for channelling the mindset in which the rider becomes focused and fired up. Not an instruction to shout

'FOCUS, you idiot FOCUS!' That would just be Parrot hijacking the PMA process.

Concentrate on What you WANT not What you Don't

It is very easy to think about what we are trying to avoid, rather than zooming in clearly on what we want. Riding to avoid mistakes, rather than to produce the best possible work. If our horse spooks we can think 'stop spooking' and attempt to suppress the movement. Or we can redirect the energy by picturing what we want the horse to do. When the horse naps we can think 'please don't rear', or we can think 'move forward'. Mouse is far more likely to anticipate, and alert you to problems, which encourages you to ride passively to avoid mistakes. Instead, have a clear image in your mind of what you want, and ride for that. Adjust your body for what you are looking or feeling for, and your horse will adjust to match you. For example, when trotting in a 2 beat, mentally feel the 3 beat rhythm of canter and you will notice your horse preparing to canter. Then just allow it to happen. If you are trotting and your horse shies in the corner, don't fixate on the shy or the corner; maintain focus on the feel of the trot you are after.

Exercises to Develop Trust and Feel

We tend to change what we do when the jumps get bigger, as Player 1 simply does not trust Player 2 to manage. But trust is far more important than try.

Jump at a height that feels comfortable. Pay attention to the canter quality, to where you are looking, and to the lines. Let the fences come to you. Feel the horse's movements. Once the round is flowing nicely, lock in that feeling, increase the heights, and ride in exactly the same way, with exactly the same feel. Still looking ahead, still aware of canter quality and so on. We can often change how we ride when the jumps go up, which means we ride higher fences less effectively than smaller ones. This is entirely counter-productive.

Place a small straight on a circle. Canter the circle, popping the jump each time. Look at the helper on the ground, in the centre of the circle, not at the jump. You will realise that, even though you are not looking at the jump, you are still aware of it. This helps build trust that you don't need to look AT fences to know where they are, and to feel when the horse will jump.

Trot a circle and keep half-halting to collect back to walk. Feel when the horse is about to break. Don't ask for walk, just allow it and feel when the horse is about to make that gait shift. How accurate can you be? Try again and see if you become better at feeling this. Once you can reliably tell exactly when the horse is about to break, ask a stride earlier to maintain the trot. Repeat going from canter, then collecting back to trot.

If your horse tends to break to trot round turns when you ask for collection, then you need to get better at feeling those moments, so you can maintain canter.

Hum or Chant the Rhythm

A twist on the Chimp Taming advice of singing, is to feel what rhythm you want and then hum it. Establish a good canter and hum that rhythm. If the canter changes, your humming will change too and alert you to the change long before your conscious brain has noticed. In this way you can be more attuned to subtle changes and make continuous adjustments. You can also use this through transitions. Alternatively, you can say a 3 beat word for canter like prosecco, prosecco, prosecco. Chanting the word to the rhythm of canter will make it more obvious when you lose rhythm.

Feel movement as fluid not sequential. Horses in a field are not going: walk-transition-trot-transition-canter-transition-trot. They are just seamlessly shifting from one gait to another, one rhythm to another, with no brace or hitch. Hum a 2 beat in trot, then switch to a 4 beat for walk or a 3 beat for canter. You are not thinking trot-transition-walk. But simply feeling 2 beat, then feeling 4 beat and back up to 2 beat.

Summary

This chapter completes our journey round the mental menagerie. Chimp, Parrot and Mouse represent many of the issues affecting riders, and those pursuing other sports. Learning how to tame the Chimp, shoot the Parrot and silence the Mouse is truly transformative, not just in sport but also in life.

CHAPTER 9

Winning Behaviours

How you do anything is how you do everything

This is a deceptively simple idea but a powerful one. People who are very successful embody the behaviours that make them successful in different aspects of their lives. They don't just put on 'winning behaviours' for a few hours a week, while training.

Another way of expressing this sort of idea is Tik Maynard's concept of 'The Olympics of Everything', which he describes in his wonderful book, *In the Middle are the Horsemen*. He writes: 'There is an Olympics for dressage, eventing and show-jumping, but what would the Olympics of saddling be? What would be the four-star of trailer-loading?'

You can extend that idea to include the Olympics of driving to the yard. What is the best possible mindset for approaching your session? What would the Olympics of mounting, schooling or debriefing look like?

If that sounds a bit over the top for someone who might want to give a BE80, or a novice test, a go one day, I don't mean that you need to live the life of a dedicated athlete; tee-total and hitting the gym 4 times a week. What I mean is bringing that 'Olympics of Everything' mindset to your riding, while you are with your horse. And to everything else in your life. A mindset of positivity, focus, enthusiasm, and a choice to be truly present for all activities, is not just something you can do, but a way you can *be*.

Consider the following scene:

You've been online too long and suddenly it is 4:30 when you are meant to be riding at 5. The twin demons of procrastination and urgency mean you've wasted the afternoon, and are now rushing. You jump in the car thinking 'it only takes 12 minutes to get to the yard.' Not really acknowledging that it takes 12 minutes on a good day. 14 on an average day and up to 20 in traffic. Which there is on a Saturday afternoon. You hit a jam and you fume, enraged by temporary lights (bloody council), a learner driver (bloody learner drivers). You arrive at 4.55. You march up to the field, your horse sees you coming and buggers off. 15 minutes later, he's let you catch him, and you tack up. Damn, you've forgotten that new bit you were lent and advised to try at your last lesson. Never mind, next time. You are riding by 5:20 – with the arena booked until 6. You don't have a session planned, so you just do whatever comes to mind as you're riding.

Purely as a result of mind set, this session was short and unstructured, the rider's behaviour in trying to catch the horse in a hurry was predatory, so he ran away. The horse was given no time to transition from rest to work. And then a tense rider tried to school a stressed horse with no focus to the session. And without the equipment that she had been asked to use by her instructor. Unsurprisingly, not a lot was achieved.

An 'Olympics of Everything' rider understands that catching and tacking up are part of training and schooling, helpful in establishing calm and harmony. She would be fully present with her horse from the moment she arrived on the yard, not late or distracted by petty irritations. She would have the session planned, and would have the correct equipment. The session would be purposeful and focused.

This approach is not only a lot more constructive, but is also far more relaxing, far more satisfying and far less stressful. Focused presence is not just better for your riding but is much more fulfilling and fun. It has nothing to do with talent. Rather, it is a simple choice to do it better. This also improves confidence, because you remove most of the stress by simply staying calmly focused and present. And you will improve much quicker too.

The pro cycling team, SKY, who were utterly dominant for many years, employed someone whose job title was 'Head of Winning Behaviours'. She was not a coach. She did not get involved in the training side of things.

Her entire focus was mindset, which is a crucial part of any sport.

Find The Fun

I recently helped a competitor who had under-performed in her previous few events. She had been very successful earlier in the season, and now had an expectation that she would win. She felt she had a target on her back. Winning mattered so much that all she could think about was the fear of not winning. Logically she understood that no-one wins all the time, not even the best riders in the world. But, emotionally, a poor placing felt catastrophic. Her nerves were so intense, and her misery so profound after underperforming, that she was contemplating giving up competing altogether.

Lots of people asked her why it mattered so much, but she just said 'I don't know, it just does.' So, instead I asked her what she loved about eventing and how she felt about her horse. Her face lit up: 'It's the camaraderie. We are all a bit mad in the eventing world and I feel accepted there. I love the feeling of doing this crazy adventure with my friends. I trust my horse, he's amazing. He looks after me. It's a real partnership. And it's *fun*.'

We came up with a PMA statement that captured those feelings for her. I asked her to focus on that feeling of fun, friendship, partnership and adventure. And to focus on absolutely nothing except that feeling. She competed 2 days later and texted me to say 'I just focused on what a great team we are, and how much fun we have. I did not think about anything else at all.'

As it happened, she won. But that really wasn't the point of the work. Success is more likely if you are relaxed and enjoying yourself, but actually the point of finding the fun is not to find the fun so you will win, but to find the fun *because that's what it is all about*. If you can chill out, and embrace the glorious pleasure of whatever sport you do, then – yes – success is more likely, but you will feel successful whether you win or not, because your primary goal is no longer winning but enjoying yourself, having fun and performing to your ability. Shift your attention to the process, not the outcome. This focus on fun was described by teenage diving sensation, Andrea Spendolini-Sirieix. After winning Commonwealth gold she said her priority had not been winning but having fun.

Tik Maynard also describes the importance of fun, while querying whether that really is a legitimate way to progress. He writes: 'Part of my passion is based on the thinking and planning side of horsemanship, but it was still, for me, a primarily physical enjoyment – the childish delight of running and jumping we rationalise through organised sport. At heart, when I rode I felt more like a happy dolphin leaping and diving.....could being a happy dolphin really be a career?'

> **KEY CONCEPT:**
> **Finding the fun makes you a better rider or athlete, and is a powerful antidote to the worrying, doubting, indecisive Mouse. Channel your inner happy dolphin!**

A Positive Attitude to 'Failure'

We live in a performance culture. Our children sit exams at aged 7. While, in theory, it is the school and not the child being evaluated, most children are aware that they are taking exams, and that they are being assessed. The concept of winning and losing, or passing and failing is conditioned in us from a young age. As a result, many of us define success or failure in very narrow ways, and we fear 'failure.'

This occurs because we view errors as failures. And we also view failures as personal, connected to failings or flaws in ourselves. We beat ourselves up for failing. This is often on the basis that people view self-criticism as the road to improvement. But it does not work. No-one gets better by telling themselves they are rubbish. It is much harder to improve if you are disheartened and deflated by errors.

Errors are events in which the actual outcome doesn't match the desired, expected or 'correct' one. Errors can lead to curiosity, exploration, critical thinking and reflection. They can lead to a willingness to try again, to try a different way, and to reconsider the problem from another angle. As such, errors can lead to creativity, flexibility, resilience, growth and greater understanding.

Failure, by contrast, is just seen as the absence of success. A loss. Entirely negative. Not surprisingly, many people try hard to avoid failure. This makes them less likely to experiment, to try new things, to see things from new perspectives, to stretch themselves or to take risks.

Matthew Syed's book, *Black Box Thinking, The Surprising Truth About Success*, explains clearly how a positive attitude to failure can lead to success in all spheres of life. He discusses ice-skating where a group of young, promising skaters were followed over a period of time. Those who made the most progress were the ones who fell most often in training. If you are willing to train near the edge of your competency and risk a 'fail' (ie a fall), then you will progress much faster than if you stay within your comfort zone. Shizuka Arakawa of Japan estimates that she fell around 20,000 times, as she progressed from a beginner to an Olympic champion.

Willingness to fail is an attitude evident in many areas of human achievement. JK Rowling had her first Harry Potter book rejected 12 times before Bloomsbury accepted it. She was also regularly rejected as Robert Galbraith, for the Cormoran Strike novels, even posting some withering responses on Twitter to encourage other writers.

In Stephen King's book, *On Writing*, he says he pinned every rejection letter he received to his wall with a nail, until there were so many that the nail was no longer big enough to hold them all up. He replaced the nail with a spike and continued trying to get his work published.

James Dyson built 5126 failed prototypes for his dual cyclone vacuum before coming up with a successful design. WD40 stands for Water Displacement 40th formula. The previous 39 were 'failures.'

Once again, Irish Eventer, Jonty Evans provides a great example, writing:

"Yes I did things wrong at times but the bulk of it was awesome and the mistakes are a LOT smaller then they were. All my career I've believed that being a good rider is about learning to cope with those mistakes. We are ALL going to make them, large or small, so we better learn to cope with them.'

In fact, *learn* from them!

KEY CONCEPT:
Being willing to try, despite the risk of failure, and being willing to learn from setbacks, is essential for anyone who wants to genuinely stretch their potential and break through self-limiting beliefs.

Daniel Coyle also talks about the importance of working at the edge of your ability in his book, *The Talent Code*. Coyle discusses the crucial role of the neural insulator, myelin, in developing skill. When we become skilled at a task, neural chains are created. Repeated practice leads to myelin wrapping around those neural chains, which increases their conductivity. Each new layer of myelin increases our skill, speed and accuracy. We are literally building 'talent' by deep practice. However, mere repetition is not enough. Once we can perform a task to a certain skill level, simply repeating that task means we move into auto-pilot, and do not create new myelin. This is why performances can plateau for long periods of time, as we repeat what we already know.

Skills come from struggle, and the discomfort of not quite getting something. Myelin is built when we are operating at the edge of our ability, and are making – and correcting – mistakes. 'Failure' can therefore lead to profound learning, if you use it constructively.

Performance Zones

You can conceptualise how far to push yourself and your horse by thinking in terms of zones. If the task is too easy you may be in the Boredom Zone. You feel confident and happy in the Comfort Zone. You make the most progress in the Learning Zone. You are a danger to yourself and your horse if you go too far beyond the level of your current ability, and enter the Panic Zone.

Horses also have these zones. If they need to build confidence, the Comfort Zone is a good place to be. To make progress, stretch them with spells in the Learning Zone. Go too far and you overwhelm them, and they enter the Panic Zone.

At a certain stress, level, you simply can't learn, as the process of learning requires deep practice in which new information is processed and understood. A horse or human operating on high alert is simply reacting to what is around them, not responding thoughtfully, and certainly not retaining anything useful. Trigger stacking is a helpful concept for ensuring that neither you nor your horse are becoming overwhelmed.

Imagine arranging to go on holiday to a cottage in the middle of nowhere. You arrive first, alone. It is dark and the weather is awful, with thick fog, driving rain and strong winds. The cottage feels creepy, as the wind howls around it. Then there is a power cut and you find yourself in the pitch dark. You hear something tapping loudly on the window, and you edge away from the noise, accidentally stumbling backwards into a coat rack. It feels to your fevered brain, that you are being engulfed by someone in a padded duvet coat. You spin round and scream. Is the problem a fear of coat racks? Is desensitizing the person to coats the way forward?

No, of course not. The coat rack was simply the final trigger that sent the person over the edge. But the conditions for fear were set by the environment: the sense of being alone, the dark, the noise of the wind and the ambiguity of a tapping noise (perhaps a tree branch) that the person could not make sense of, and therefore assumed was threatening.

The same principle applies to our horses. If they are somewhere new, if they are separated from a herd mate, if they are wearing unfamiliar tack that feels more restrictive etc, these triggers accumulate, and they will be more reactive to any additional stressor, like a sudden noise, or a 'scary' Shetland pony along the fence line. There is also not much 'head-room' left for learning new skills, if the horse is already stressed just by being that situation. It is better to stay well within his comfort zone, until the horse settles and is in a better frame of mind for learning.

I also like to conceptualise how far to push both myself and my horse in terms of credit and debit. Confidence comes from time in the Comfort Zone and you can think of this as depositing credit into the bank of confidence. You can then withdraw this credit when you go into the Learning Zone. If you make mistakes, then you will take out more credit. If improvement comes easily to you and the horse, then you don't lose much credit at all. Although mistakes are inevitable in the Learning Zone, you need to ensure that the overall balance in the confidence bank stays in credit. If you or your horse has a real issue (as we did at that dreadful eventer trial) then drop back into the Comfort Zone to add a bit more credit, before seeking to make withdrawals again.

Horses are much more tolerant of the Learning Zone if they are comfortable with learning. An important, and often overlooked, part of building a horse's confidence, and making progress, is teaching them to learn.

Finding the Try: Helping Horses Learn

It is important for us to have a positive, curious and problem-solving response to 'failure'. This is just as important for our horse. We need to get our horses feeling comfortable with making mistakes, and not being sure of the answer to a question. Many horsemanship trainers stress the importance of 'finding the try'. We want our horses to be willing to try and work out what it is that we are asking of them. We achieve this by asking a question, via a small amount of pressure, then sitting quietly while our horse offers various behaviours in response. When the horse stumbles on the right one, we release to reward a 'try' that was in the right direction.

When I first got Amber it was clear that she was used to having riders legged up onto her as she trotted down the road. Being asked to stand still was hugely confusing to her. I'd pick up the rein and just wait. She tried everything, except for standing still. She tried moving forward, sideways, shaking her head, backing up, stamping a foot. And eventually she stood still. I immediately released the rein pressure, and gave her a break. Then I picked up the reins again. Repeat, repeat, repeat till the penny dropped and she learned that picking up the rein does not mean start moving. She quickly became very good at being horse-as-sofa.

Horses learn quickly this way, but crucially they learn *how to learn*. Once a horse has understood that a release will come, then they also understand that they need to search for it, and they actively seek solutions.

When you have a step in the right direction, then you build on that first (now reliable) step by asking for a little more before the release. Perhaps now you want the horse to soften to you when you pick up the rein. On the first attempt the horse will stand still and expect a release. This time the release does not come and the horse thinks 'hey, where is my release?' Sooner or later they try something different: lean into the pressure, try to snatch the rein etc. Eventually they stumble on softening, and the pressure is released. Repeat, repeat, repeat. In this way you slowly shape the responses you want.

Clicker training works on exactly the same principle, only you add in positive reinforcement (a treat) rather than simply pressure/release, but with both approaches horses become willing to 'get it wrong' as they seek to find the 'right' answer. And once you have achieved that, then you have an actively engaged horse, willing to work with you and eager to learn.

The skill lies in knowing when and what to reward, so the horse does not learn things you are not trying to teach, (like tucking a nose in behind the bit), and getting the timing right, but a mindset of 'reward the try' is a way of setting your horses up to be willing and motivated problem-solving partners.

The opposite of a curious, engaged horse, is a horse who has learned to fear failure and has become unwilling to offer responses, in case they 'get it wrong', and are punished for their mistake. The extreme end point of this process is a horse who enters a state of 'learned helplessness'. This is a passive coping strategy in which the horse retreats into himself and shuts the world and the rider out. They don't know what you want and they are too scared to make suggestions, so they shut down or freeze. Such horses may be described as sour, evasive, lazy, stubborn or resistant.

KEY CONCEPT:
Finding and rewarding 'the try' is crucial for developing a horse's confidence and keeping them engaged and willing to learn.

This willingness to reward small steps is greatly helped by an attitude of gratitude.

Gratitude

Psychologists are becoming increasingly aware of the power of gratitude. It provides a strong defence against stress, depression, boredom, frustration and anger. Not surprisingly, it is also a powerful Parrot and Chimp antidote. In addition, the more you thank your horse, the more grateful for that your horse will be. Gratitude extended to your horse, also requires you to be supportive and kind to yourself, as the reality is that being hard on yourself is also automatically being hard on your horse, who always knows when you are angry and upset. Even if it is directed inwards.

Let's just take a step back and reflect on the extraordinary gifts our horses give us. They are born with their prey-animal instincts fully intact. We are predators and they know it. Everything about our shape tells them that: eyes directly in front to track prey, movements direct and purposeful, predatory in our behaviours and eye-contact. When you are on horse-back you can often ride quite close to deer as they see the horses as nonthreatening. Try approaching deer on 2 feet and you won't see them for dust.

We insist that horses subject themselves to our touch, and that they allow us to take away their ability to flee by handling their feet. We stable them when they instinctively seek out open spaces. We put a head collar on them to further restrain and restrict them. All this is completely alien to a foal. Then we strap dead animal hides onto their backs, right where predators jump, and put metal in their mouths. Then we get on them and want them to carry us, and go where we tell them.

It is absolutely extraordinary that sensitive flight animals, like horses, allow this. Some don't, and those few who simply never accept riders remind us that no horse has to accept a rider. Any horse could put any human on the ground any time they choose. Mostly, however, they don't.

And then what? We don't just expect them to carry us on relaxed ambles round the countryside. We expect them to perform for us. They need to walk, trot and canter holding themselves and moving in the ways we humans have decided 'matters' or is 'correct'. We expect them to understand that the leg can mean stand, back, forward, sideways, bend, turn, collect or extend. At the same time, we expect them to filter out the many times the leg means nothing at all, and is just unstable rider 'noise'. And don't even ask me to explain what the rein can do, as I am not sure even I know, but I expect my horse to know.

Then we expect them to jump, when it makes so much more sense to go around. I wonder what they would say if they could talk?

'You want me to go OVER'
'Yes please'
'But there's loads of space either side'
'I know that, but please go over'

'It's much more effort to go over'

'But that's what I want'

'I can't see the other side. Or what's in the middle of the thing I'm jumping over'

'Do it anyway'

'Even that super skinny massive brush thing I can barely fit over'

'Yup'

'Can I just have a quick look at it?'

'NO! GO NOW, NOW!'

And then when it comes to show-jumping, just getting over is not good enough, They have to go over without touching anything. Even though they have no idea why that matters.

We also expect them to do those random 'correct' movements, and jump over lots of things for no evident reason, in a busy, buzzy show atmosphere. They have to deal with flappy tents, tannoys, lorries. They have to go into a horse warm-up area then leave all their new friends behind to head for the dressage where there are no other horses. Then they have to stay focused, relaxed, calm and obedient. They need to be Goldilocks and Mary Poppins rolled into one: Not too fast and not too slow but just right. Practically perfect in every way: submissive and obedient the *instant* we ask them for a change.

We would never expect that from our own children. No 'wait a minute' or 'can I just quickly have a quick look at?' or 'what's that over there?' No calling out to friends. No wiggling or fidgeting, adjusting position or stretching to relieve discomfort. No running on ahead, exploring a leaf in a puddle or lagging behind allowed. No curiosity, anxiety, checking things out, exuberance, feet dragging or expressing any kind of opinion or preference is tolerated when schooling or competing.

And they do it. These remarkable animals do it. Yet we label their mistakes as lazy, rude, disobedient, stupid, wilful. Even if we don't, but blame ourselves instead, the horse knows we are unhappy and frustrated. We can take responsibility for errors, but we are still communicating: NOT HAPPY. The horse understands that we are unhappy, whether we like it or not. If we are hard on ourselves, we are automatically equally hard on our horse.

So maybe next time you are disappointed that your horse was tense in the dressage, jogged in the walk, missed the marker for the transition down to trot, rolled a pole in the show-jumping or needed a 2nd look at a funny looking fence into water, just pause, and maybe, just maybe, stroke or scratch his wither, and say 'that's fine, well tried.' Focus on all the amazing things he *does* do for you, instead of being frustrated about the moments of doubt, confusion, uncertainly, tension, carelessness or exuberance. And do the same for your own errors or lapses of concentration.

Horses are not robots. They are exquisitely sensitive, generous, brave and willing flight animals, who don't have to do a damn thing for us, but actually do. And the best bit about a mindset of gratitude, is that treating our horse like he's a winner, and has done incredibly well, regardless of the areas that still need work, makes you feel like a winner too. Try replacing frustration with gratitude. Find something to thank him sincerely for. Keeping you safe? Getting you round? Trying his best? A nice centre-line? A relaxed warm-up? Easy to handle? Tolerant of wind or rain? Something. Then extend that same mentality to yourself. Praise yourself for trying hard, taking a risk, turning your horse out beautifully, an improved dressage score, a positive attitude to an elimination. Anything! If you sincerely thank your horse, and cultivate an attitude of gratitude, while also giving yourself credit for your own efforts, this will eventually feel more automatic, and will carry over to your post event or post lesson reflections. These reflections will therefore be more positive and balanced. This approach is not arrogant or complacent. It is a mindset that leads to greater acceptance, balanced self-appraisal and a constructive plan moving forward. It fosters positivity and hope.

Being critical of your horse, or down on yourself, leads to despondency and irritation, which get you nowhere.

> **KEY CONCEPT:**
> **An attitude of gratitude is far better for**
> **both of you.**

In Praise of Pointlessness: Understanding how Privileged We are

During iron distance training I was once on a windy 5 hour bike ride which took me past the picturesque and lively village of Alderley Edge. I saw lots of people sitting at pavement cafes, drinking espressos and reading the papers. Like I could be if I wasn't fool enough to be training for such a tough event. The question 'what am I doing an ironman for anyway?' popped into my head. Simple enough question. No immediate answer came readily to mind. Since I still had about 4 hours to kill on my bike, and not much else to think about, I decided to try and figure it out. It then further occurred to me that the very LAST place and time I should be thinking about the 'point' of ironman was on a windy 5 hour bike ride.

However, the word 'point' stuck in my mind. As in 'what's the point.' It seemed self-evidently true that endurance events – in fact all sports – are fundamentally pointless. But then so is pretty much any human endeavour not solely geared to survival and procreation. If we only did things that had a point, we would never paint a picture, create music, climb mountains, gallop along a beach or go eventing.

I'm no anthropologist but I wonder if one of the things that truly separates humans, from all other creatures, is that we do things for absolutely no reason at all. We embrace pointlessness. Our engagement in pointlessness is what makes us human. Animals 'play', but they do so to learn and practice survival skills. Only a human being would create a replica battleship out of 1,000,000 matchsticks, create works of art, or train for pointless athletic endeavours.

In places of total poverty, life becomes pared to its essentials. Wake, work to earn enough to eat, eat, sleep……repeat. That is a desperate kind of life. Similarly, depression can be characterised by the gradual erosion of everything 'pointless', such as films, galleries, walks, socialising – and training for pointless athletic endeavours. Until life becomes more and more focused on scraping by.

I have always been the kind of person who likes having challenges and goals. It doesn't really matter what those goals are. So yes, ironman is pointless. Eventing is pointless. Showing is pointless. Dressage is pointless. Art and music are pointless. And our uniquely human ability to celebrate and embrace pointlessness is totally life affirming at the same time.

KEY CONCEPT:
It helps to maintain gratitude when we recognise how privileged we are.

CHAPTER 10

Acceptance

The final piece in the mindset puzzle is recognising that you have the power to be happy. Whether you compete or not. Whether you place or not. With whatever horse you have, or whatever hobby or sport you choose. The secret to this peaceful, joyful state of mind is acceptance.

The Acceptance Pyramid

There is a simple and highly effective way of thinking about what 'acceptance' means in practice. It profoundly differs from resistance and resentment, and it is possible to cultivate an attitude of acceptance, in even the most challenging of situations.

Imagine something has happened that you are very unhappy about. Let's say your farrier shod your horse badly causing nail bind, and he is now lame. Or you have failed to qualify for a Championship by a single placing, and you have video evidence you were given 20 penalties unfairly for a stop at the water. Or someone borrowed your wheelbarrow without asking, and damaged it.

Option A is changing the situation. This is the preferred option. You could use practical problem-solving strategies and do things like:

- Ask the farrier to correct the error
- Contact the event with the video footage
- Speak to the yard owner or other liveries, to see if you can find out who damaged the wheelbarrow, so they can pay for repairs.

But these solutions don't always work:

- The farrier replaces the shoe, but the horse remains lame
- The event says you lodged your complaint too late, and rejects your request for the result to be changed
- The yard owner and liveries are not concerned about your wheelbarrow, and there is no evidence pointing in any particular direction

If you cannot change the situation, you can turn to Option 2: Changing how you feel about it.

Using the concepts in this book, you could try and be more balanced and rational in your view of events.

For example:

- Instead of 'that farrier deserves to be shot, how dare he, it's so unfair', you could think 'farriers are only human, nail bind is common, the horse will be fine in the end.'
- Instead of outrage that your result will not be changed, you could think 'fence judges are only volunteers, no-one was out to get me personally.'
- Instead of being infuriated about the wheelbarrow you could think 'no wheelbarrow lasts forever, it could easily have been damaged when I next used it myself. It was old and not worth getting upset over.'

Sometimes this can help to a degree, but we are likely to still be left with some frustration, disappointment and sadness, even if Option 2 has taken the edge off our distress. We can then choose to take Option 3: ACCEPT IT.

Acceptance means acknowledging how you feel, and then letting go and moving on. This creates a much healthier mindset than ruminating on it endlessly, and telling yourself an 'it's unfair, why did this happen, it's not right' story.

If you are unwilling to accept it (which is a CHOICE) then you move automatically to Option 4: stay miserable about it. This is the place of resistance and resentment. You have the right to stay here. After all, what happened was not your fault, and is genuinely upsetting. But what good does it do you to stay here?

In some situations, people might even move to Option 5: Make the situation worse. If you kick off at your farrier, or the event organizer, they may bar you. If you make too much of a meal of the damage to your wheelbarrow, the yard owner and other liveries may get fed up with you, and so you lose friends and feel less welcome. These adverse outcomes make what was already a challenging situation, even worse.

People who deal with events using options 1-3 have the power to stay positive and calm. An attitude of acceptance allows them to be as happy as the situation permits, no matter what has happened. Living this way is profoundly life-enhancing. You can be happy, despite pain, if you calmly expect and accept that sometimes things hurt, physically or emotionally.

In *The Chimp Paradox*, Dr Steve Peters talks about 'The Truths of Life'. His most fundamental truths are:

1) Life is not fair
2) The goal posts move
3) Nothing is guaranteed

In practice this means he expects and *accepts* unfairness, moving goal posts and the lack of any guarantees. If he can hold these fundamental truths in mind, very little will upset him.

We generally expect life to be fair. But a moment's thought reveals this expectation to be utterly illogical. Some people are born into palaces, some into small, damp flats and some into homelessness. Some people live to 100 and are hale and hearty all their lives, others are plagued with illness and disability, then die young. Mistakes are made by every human in every job, so some people will be misdiagnosed, some will be sent to prison when they are innocent, some will be blamed for other people's errors by managers making a mistake. We can aspire to be fair ourselves, and we can hope for fairness from others, and from the universe, but *expecting* it, will make your miserable.

A willingness to accept reality is useful in all circumstances, from the mildly irritating, to the truly catastrophic. This attitude is exemplified by the eventer, Nicola Wilson, who sustained life changing injuries at Badminton in 2022. I have mentioned Nicola earlier, as I had lessons with her before her accident. She is an inspirational coach, and is equally inspirational now, as a living embodiment of acceptance and positivity, despite unimaginably challenging circumstances.

In the blink of an eye, Nicola went from being an elite athlete, aiming for World Championships and Olympic medals, to someone who could no longer realistically ride. Even when still in hospital, Nicola accepted the reality of her situation, without an ounce of self-pity or resentment evident. In vlogs posted online from hospital, she celebrated triumphs such as lifting a fork to her mouth, and bearing weight for the first time. She faced her new world with clear-eyed courage, and has created exciting new ambitions to use her vast knowledge, and world class facilities, to mentor and support the next generation of riders aiming for elite levels.

Acceptance does not mean skipping around as if everything is rosy, while suppressing or ignoring deep feelings of loss, grief and sadness about awful circumstances and events. It is healthy to allow yourself to feel the enormity of the changes and losses thrust upon you. Honouring and allowing those feelings fully is part of acceptance. Much resistance results from a refusal to allow yourself to feel what you feel. This is often a way of avoiding grief, in favour of anger and bitterness, which can feel easier to tolerate. Railing against the world for an injustice is often less painful than facing up to what has actually happened. But that response leads to greater, and more prolonged suffering, in the long run.

My first child was a healthy, full-term baby, but complications in labour meant he was born critically ill. He had inhaled sticky meconium deep into his lungs during labour, which formed a physical barrier. Not enough oxygen was getting from the lungs into his blood. Throughout the first night of his life, I simply refused to accept this. I argued with doctors, I shouted at nurses. One doctor said they did not want to ventilate him because that could cause additional problems. When he came back to tell me that my son was now being ventilated, I was angry and demanded to know why they had done something that might hurt him, refusing to listen to the very obvious 'because we reached the point where we had no choice' answer. I simply could not accept a reality in which my baby was going to die. (Just to reassure readers, he lived and is a healthy 20 year old, as I write.)

But at the time he was gravely ill, and in the early hours of the morning after he was born we were summoned to his incubator on the NICU to say goodbye. At that moment I let go of resistance and accepted we were losing him. I allowed myself to feel the emotions I had avoided through yelling angrily at staff all night. I felt crushing sadness and aching loss. I also felt love. Love between me and my son, and between me and my husband. I felt compassion from the doctors and nurses, who were silently holding vigil with us. I felt awe at his tiny hands and feet. I felt a lot of things, and they weren't all bad.

As it happened, a doctor suddenly, quietly said: 'is it my imagination, or is he looking a bit pinker?' Somehow, shortly before he would have died, he had cleared some meconium from his lungs to allow a bit more oxygen through. The crisis was averted as soon as I dropped resistance, my emotions transformed from anger and denial, to love, compassion and grief. This was a powerful example of the healing potential of acceptance.

Resistance arises when we are faced with realities we wish were different, and leads to suffering and stuckness. We can't plan new goals, and a new way of living that adjusts for changes and losses, if we won't accept them. We can't be pleased with achievements and steps forward, if we refuse to accept that activities we used to take for granted are now hugely challenging.

Nicola Wilson's vlogs from hospital show her accepting the reality of her situation with composure, humour and courage. With that mindset, she is able to celebrate achievements and milestones, instead of living in a parallel universe where she can still do these things without effort. And she is able to plan new ventures, and build new dreams, rather than focusing on what she is no longer able to do.

> **KEY CONCEPT:**
> **Accepting life as it truly is, as opposed to how you would like it to be, allows for growth and positive transformations. Resentment and resistance leads to bitterness and stagnation.**

Acceptance can also help people tolerate physical discomfort. We are biologically conditioned to avoid pain, and to resent it when it arrives. The Chimp can't see the point of pain, regarding it as threatening, and seeking to avoid it, or escape from it. But many ambitious challenges that excite and inspire us humans, require tolerance of high levels of pain. In these events, success or failure is predicted by mindset far more than by physical fitness. I have been in more pain, but suffered far less, than many people also taking part in ultra-endurance events. Some people quit with tired, sore feet. Others complete with broken ones!

Happiness Despite Pain

If I had to choose 1 endurance challenge that stands out it would be the Jurassic Coastal Challenge. 80 off-road and ludicrously hilly miles, split over 3 consecutive days along my favourite stretch of coastline: the Dorset Coastal Path between Lyme Regis & Studland.

Training for the challenge felt fantastic. It was the coldest winter for years, but it was often clear and bright. A triple marathon was a leap into the unknown, so I saw training as preparation for mental toughness as much as for physical fitness. A race at the end of March could involve almost any kind of weather, from freakishly warm to extremely wintry. As such, I relished wind and rain, hail, sleet and snow. 'Could be like this on race day', became my new mantra. Some of the training highlights were breaking trail in deep snow shortly after sunrise on Shining Tor and a training weekend on outrageous hills in Dorset in January.

The race itself feels indescribable. How to capture the magnitude and the variety of the experiences. The lifetimes in a single race. Over 80 miles and over 20 hours of thigh burning climbing and leg shredding descending; of stunning scenery with sun beams dancing on breath-taking sweeping bays; of wild weather with hail, wind, impenetrable mist, suddenly parting to reveal vertigo inducing, crumbling cliffs. Of exhaustion and exhilaration, of peaceful solitude and crushing loneliness. Of sociable camaraderie and friendships forged in shared endeavour. Of pain and pride. And of finishing. Crossing that line. And knowing that anything, truly, is possible.

It was clear throughout the event that I was physically weaker than many people who quit. And also that I was positive and focused when others were miserable, even though we were all hurting. It showed me that while pain is inevitable, suffering is optional. A concept explained beautifully by Mo Gawdat in his book, *Solve for Happy*. Unhappiness comes largely from perceptions and expectations of events not the events themselves. I was definitely hurting but I was not suffering.

KEY CONCEPT:
Pain is inevitable. Suffering is optional.

This idea is also explored in much more detail in Zen Master, Cheri Huber's life changing book, *Suffering Is Optional: Three Keys to Freedom and Joy.* This book centres around three basic aspects of Zen practice: pay attention, believe nothing, and don't take anything personally. All very powerful anti-Parrot advice.

Around 65 miles into the Jurassic Coastal Challenge, at the top of some brutally steep and long steps, there is a memorial bench. The inscription reads: 'Time Passes. LISTEN! Time passes.'

'Time passes' has long been a mantra of mine, for when I am digging deep in whatever challenge I am doing. I read the first 2 words with a smile of recognition, assuming it meant 'these steps and hills won't go on forever. One step at a time, don't worry this will be over soon.' But the next 3 words hit me: LISTEN! Time Passes. What was I missing? What did I need to listen to? Why the urgency? It struck me that Time Passes is also a call to recognise that life is precious and fleeting. The person the memorial was dedicated to is no longer with us. It seemed a call to not just survive the moment, but to embrace it. To wake up, be present and LIVE. I sat on the bench and looked at the most spectacular view over the cliffs to the sea. And, despite the pain, the bone-deep exhaustion, and the remaining 15 very hilly miles to the finish, I was truly happy.

The realisation that you can be happy while freezing cold, exhausted and in pain; and you can be miserable on a beach in the Bahamas, has implications for everything in life, including how much joy you get from your horses. Happiness can be found wherever you are. As can misery.

Key Concept:
Experiences don't make you happy or unhappy.
Perceptions and expectations do.

This is a powerful truth and fully embracing it will transform your life. Experiences don't make you happy. There is no doubt some experiences make you UN-happy – you cannot be happy if you are being held captive with your family and watching them be hurt. But extremes aside, you can be perfectly happy in difficult circumstances, and utterly miserable in favourable ones. Just as you can feel strong connections with others while on your own, and lonely in a crowd.

My most recent example of happiness in difficult circumstances was my first one day event on my new horse, Lottie. I had no expectations of how we would go, and so anything other than elimination would have felt like a win.

I went in expecting some show-jumping and cross-country faults. When she went double-clear I felt like we could jump the moon. Reality was so much better than my expectations had been. My perception was that she was a brave, beautiful, brilliant mare, and I was so excited, happy and proud.

So I was happy. Very, very happy.

However, I also had a broken car, and was a couple of hundred miles from home, with no rescue coverage for Lottie. I had to put out an emergency call on social media for a horse transporter, pay them an eye watering amount to rescue her, and arrange for someone to meet her at the other end, as I had to go with the car. I had to wait around for hours for them to fetch her. Then I had to wait for the low-loader to flat-bed us the long journey home. Made even longer by HGV driving rules that meant our driver had to have a 45 minute break, less than 10 miles from home. Despite all those hassles, any one of which would normally have had me stressed, bored, frustrated and upset, nothing could dent my happiness or remove the silly grin on my face, as I savoured the reality that 'we went double-clear, WE WENT DOUBLE-CLEAR!'

The reverse is also true. There can be times when all external conditions are fine. I could be on a beach on holiday basking in sunshine, next to a sparkling sea. And yet still feel down or irritable, if my expectations are entirely unreasonable. The expectation that the wind will never go above a gentle breeze, that others on the beach will be quiet, that we will have plenty of space, that we will get a favourable parking spot, that queues for ice creams are not too long, that I don't get sand in my sandwiches. In that kind of mood, reality will never match my ludicrously demanding expectations, and I will be dissatisfied or unhappy.

Is it not experiences that are the problem, it is the expectations we place on reality and on ourselves that cause us unhappiness and stress. We can reduce these expectations by accepting reality, exactly as it is in each moment. Enjoying the good, accepting the less good, and showing resilience and courage when things are very challenging. The key to that kind of present moment acceptance is mindfulness: present moment awareness without judgement. In practice this means dealing with situations using options 1-3. Not spending time in the misery of resentment and bitterness, or actually making your situation even worse by your reactions to adversity.

People may think of mindfulness as sitting on a cushion, counting breaths, or taking 3 minutes to eat a raisin. These are indeed very useful ways to experience mindfulness. But I actually found that endurance sport works beautifully as a mindfulness exercise. This may have something to do with the utter simplicity of it. There is a pair of legs or a bike. There is a hill and a distance to be covered, at the end of which are rest and shelter. The equation is very clear. You need to get over the hill and cover the distance. You need to deal with whatever the ride or run is throwing at you in order to get home. You learn very quickly that there is absolutely no point getting stressed about things like weather, tiredness or mechanical problems. You may have to deal with storms and other problems to get home. Thinking: 'it's not fair, and why is it so damn windy in Derbyshire, and I can't believe it's raining AGAIN, and I'm too cold and it's too far and why the hell didn't I get the train or take a mobile' is just going to wind you up and wear you down. And at the end of the internal tantrum you still have to ride or run home.

Instead, endurance athletes learn to accept the situation as it is and just ride on home. This is a perfect example of practicing equanimity, patience and acceptance of things as they are, rather than wasting energy on wishing they were other than as they are. These are the roots of mindfulness. It is an extremely useful philosophy for anyone looking after horses in winter in the UK. Or anyone competing a mud loving white pony..... (Me and, er, me). Exactly the same process arises in all areas of life, but the apparent complexity of modern living hides the obvious truth, that rejection of reality, as it actually is, leads to suffering.

What, So What, Now What

Horseman, Mark Rashid, describes a way of processing frustrating or challenging situations, that he found helpful in staying focused and solution oriented. He credits his horse, Buck, for teaching him this. He noticed that whenever something unexpected or unwanted happened, he (Mark) would get lost in frustration, cursing the situation, and blaming himself or his horse. In one example, he was herding cows and he spooked one by moving too fast. The entire herd disappeared, meaning several extra hours of work. While Mark was ranting to the universe about how annoying and unfair this was, Buck quietly went back to work. Over time, Mark realised that the suffering and stress is in the ranting. The situation itself is just something that needs to be dealt with. You can deal with it calmly, or you can tell yourself a sob story, but that won't save you any time. The ranting actually makes you more annoyed, frustrated, or despondent about the mistake you or your horse made, than the situation itself.

Mark said Buck had an attitude of What? So what? Now what?

'What' refers to a clear-eyed understanding of what has happened. In Rashid's anecdote, the cows have vanished down the valley in the wrong direction. It could be your trailer getting stuck in the mud, or a fall in the dressage warm-up of a one day event, meaning elimination before you have even started, or a brand new phone that you have dropped and broken.

'So what' refers to the implication of what has happened. What does that mean for me right now? For Rashid, the implication was several extra hours in the saddle to retrieve the lost herd, and direct them back to where they should have been. He claims that Buck was a fantastic horse and knew his job inside out. Buck understood that the cows had gone the wrong way, and that meant many more hours work. In fact, he anticipated their break for freedom, as Mark was moving too fast, and very uncharacteristically ignored his first few cues to go even faster. But Mark – believing he knew better – insisted, and so Buck sped up, and the cows reacted.

If your trailer is stuck, you need to alert someone at the event and wait to be towed out. If you have fallen off, it means you can't continue with the competition. If you have broken your phone, then you can either buy a new one, use your old one or live without one.

'Now what' refers to a calm acceptance of those implications and an 'ok let's get on with it' attitude. 'Now what' might be active: Ok let's fetch those cows. Ok my competition is over, so I better drive home. Ok I need to buy another phone. Or the 'Now what' might require serene acceptance that you just need to wait for a resolution: Ok I need to wait to be towed out. And sometimes calm acceptance involves a recognition that the situation is as it, whether you like it or not and sometimes you can't do anything to change that. Resenting this and focusing on an alternative parallel reality, where things turned out differently, just leads to additional resentment and distress. Sometimes the best things you can do is to simply 'chuck it in the f- it bucket', let go, and move on.

Mark says Buck understood the 'So What' of the situation clearly and began executing the 'Now What': moving towards the herd without hesitation or resistance, while Mark wasted time and energy berating himself.

This is a good example of the different ways you can frame or think about your problem: The Blame Frame or the Aim Frame. Blame Frame thinking involves working out who messed up, getting angry, and possibly even seeking to punish whoever was responsible for the problem. Including punishing yourself in the form of self-criticism and frustration that you direct inwards.

Other people accept that whatever has happened has happened, and the only thing under their control is how they respond to it. This is the 'Aim Frame'. Aim Frame thinking involves simply accepting what happened, and problem solving from there, without getting lost in judgement, resentment or anger.

> **KEY CONCEPT:**
> **Mindfulness means calm acceptance of reality.**
> **Things are as they are right now, even if you**
> **would prefer them to be different.**

We are generally happy when we are mindful. Living at the crossroads of right here and right now, the only place where reality ever unfolds. Fully engaged in the moment, not fretting about the past, evaluating the present, or worrying about the future. Just embracing each moment as it arises.

When are we at our happiest? Normally this is a place above thought when we just *are*. Downhill skiing at one with the mountain, riding cross-country in harmony with our horse, laughing till we cry with our friends, walking in nature, fully absorbed in the sights and sounds around us.

Children are naturally more mindful than adults. They live joyfully in the moment, fully present, engaged and absorbed. The average 4-year-old laughs 300 times a day. The average 40-year-old laughs 4 times. We can try and rediscover that childlike wonder, that simplicity and joy, by letting go of Mouse, Chimp and Parrot, and simply living with enthusiasm and excitement. Channelling our inner 12-year-old.

Just Say Yes

Kids say yes to all sorts of stuff, all the time. Then we grow up and question everything. What-iffing and catastrophising, till we are barely able to make any decisions at all.

Recklessness is not necessarily the best life-plan, but equally neither is being overly cautious. As far as anyone is aware, this is our one life. Why not LIVE it?

William Micklem, Equestrian Coach, supports this idea with his 'Go Rules'. Which can really be summed up in Rules 1 and 2, which are Have a Go and Have Another Go. The rest support the first 2, with rules about goal setting and positive self-talk.

Outside of the equestrian world, Just Say Yes is gloriously, if madly, epitomised by Dave Cornthwaite, adventurer and founder of the SayYesMore movement.

EVERY TIME YOU DO SOMETHING NEW YOU GROW
AND SEEING AS YOU'RE HUMAN
ABLE TO ASPIRE AND THINK AND DREAM
DON'T YOU THINK IT WOULD BE SILLY
TO MISS OUT ON A CHANCE TO
MAKE LIFE MORE MEMORABLE
TO DO WHAT YOU LOVE. TO CREATE
BE AMBITIOUS & ADVENTUROUS
& MAKE EVERY MOMENT COUNT
LIVE SIMPLY. BELIEVE. START NOW
SAY YES MORE

When I was at University I joined the climbing club where I met a girl who invited me on an Arctic expedition. She was from an adventuring, Duke of Edinburgh, mountaineering kind of a background. I decidedly wasn't. My idea of an adventure was walking along the coastal path for an ice-cream.

I smoked and never exercised beyond carrying a rucksack to the base of a climb. This was not much of a recommendation for hardcore outdoor pursuits, but never-the-less I was asked along on the basis that I was agreeable enough company and didn't whinge. Important, apparently if you have to share one small tent with 2 others for 10 weeks. And I'd done 3 years at medical school which apparently equipped me to be 'camp doctor'. Finally, there was some sponsorship to be had by taking novices to the Arctic. In that part of my job description, I excelled! The expedition leader and other expeditioners were only 19, but had already been on 2 previous Arctic trips, so I was in good hands, even though I was personally clueless beyond belief.

I was hopelessly, ludicrously, under-prepared for the challenge. The expedition was self organised, and unsupported. Our kit was airdropped on a glacier Somewhere Inland. We were dropped off Somewhere On The Coast by boat. Another boat would pick us up Somewhere Else, A Very Long Way Away, 10 weeks later.

In between the long trekking, the load carrying and the Nordic skiing to get about the place, we climbed mountains. That first day demanded a 17 hour hike to find our stuff, and was one of the most miserable days of my life. I was terrified of what I had got myself into. The boat had chugged off leaving us alone. Utterly alone. We started to walk inland – a walk that re-defined the word 'heavy' as applied to rucksacks. And re-defined the words 'long' and 'hard' as applied to exercise. I seriously contemplated chucking myself down a scree slope, or shutting a razor-sharp penknife on my hand, to get myself sent home. Until I realised that I was 'camp doc' and therefore in charge of the terrifyingly complex array of medical equipment deemed necessary to keep 9 undergraduates safe for 10 weeks on our own. Kit included chest drains, morphine, leg casts and, yes, plenty of stitching materials. Assuming I didn't actually kill myself, all that would happen if I threw myself off a cliff, would be that it would be my job to patch myself up again and carry on.

I honestly don't remember the first 2 weeks. It felt like a deeply horrible and inescapable mistake. Apparently, I functioned fairly normally but I was deep in 'survival mode' and just got through each effortful day with the mantra 'time passes' playing endlessly through my mind. Then 2 weeks into the trip it felt as if I had suddenly emerged from a cocoon, and the sun had come out. I felt immeasurably stronger and fitter. The numbing fog in my head lifted and I became increasingly enthralled by the astonishing beauty of our environment. Each day had a wonderful simplicity. No contact with the outside world at all. No jobs, mail, phone calls, traffic, crowds, noise, hassle, decisions. Just skiing and climbing and climbing and skiing, day after day, week after week.

In retrospect this was a fully immersive, long-term mindfulness retreat. And it was the most profoundly, joyful and satisfying experience of my life.

Among the many things the Arctic taught me: (such as don't drop your only boots while river crossing, pilchard tins make surprisingly good ski bindings, don't forget the cap when inserting a cannula unless you want to spray blood liberally over everything), the most useful lesson was that if the mind can cope, the body has no problems. Calm acceptance of reality forms a crucial element of any pursuit. You can be deeply happy while also in significant pain and slogging through adversity. And that 'just saying yes', chucking yourself in at the deep end, participating fully, and grabbing opportunities with both hands, can sometimes take you to magical and unforgettable places.

Final Thoughts

Once upon a time there was a little girl who dreamed of one day having a pony of her very own. She spent many hours dreaming of watching her pony playing in the field. She dreamed of feeding him polos and giving him pony cuddles. She dreamed of grooming and plaiting, making her pony gorgeous and shiny. She dreamed of sitting in his stable, listening to the sound of him munching hay. She dreamed of beach rides, and hacks along the river. She dreamed of galloping and jumping. She dreamed of competing.

These dreams took a very, very long time to come true. But one day that little girl (who was not so little anymore) finally got a pony of her very own. She was able to watch him playing in the field. She fed him polos and gave him pony cuddles. She groomed and plaited him, making him gorgeous and shiny. She listened to him munching hay. She rode him on the beach and hacked him along the river. They galloped and jumped cross-country. They competed.

But by then the little girl had grown up. And each dream she achieved never seemed quite enough. Someone else's pony was always shinier. Someone else was always jumping bigger, hacking more, competing more successfully. Wherever she got to, she wanted to be just a little further along. Until she got there too, and then that did not feel quite enough either.

Then those dreams became chores. Field checks and hay-nets. Plaiting and schooling. Riding in the rain. Those adventures became scary ordeals. Competing became a source of stress and pressure.

What would that little girl – who dreamed for so long for exactly the life she now had – think of her grown up self? What would she say to the adult version of her who was too bogged down in doubt, negativity, comparisons and fear, too busy and too distracted to really enjoy her horse and her riding?

I need my inner 9 year-old to remind me to replace doubt, fear and negativity with trust, gratitude and joy. And to remember that I am literally living the dream. Right now. Are you?

My clever, curious, brave Lottie, after Chatsworth Arena Eventing.

I'd like to thank all my readers for coming along on this ride with me. I hope you had as much fun as I did and learned something you can use. If so, please consider visiting Amazon and leaving a short review. And please tell a friend!

If you have any suggestions, concerns or complaints about the book, please feel free to email me with feedback on
krissie@ivings.co.uk

To be kept updated about special offers, new camp dates, additional events, Webinars and any new releases, then please head over to
facebook.com/confidencecoachNorthwest
Like and follow the page for the latest information.

You can also stay in touch via my website:
www.aspireequestrian.co.uk

Or get all the info direct to your in-box by subscribing to my mailing list using the following link. You can unsubscribe easily anytime.
https://dashboard.mailerlite.com/forms/360416/82364
966316803617/share

Recommended Reading

Cheri Huber: *Suffering Is Optional: Three Keys to Freedom and Joy, (2002) Keep it Simply Books*

Daniel Coyle: *The Talent Code (2020); Generic.*

David Cornthwaite: *Board Free, (2018); Portico.*

Tim Gallwey: *The Inner Game of Tennis (2014), Pan Books.*

Mo Gawdat: *Solve for Happy: Engineer Your Path to Joy, (2017); Bluebird*

Tik Maynard: *In the Middle are the Horsemen. (2018) Trafalgar Square Books*

Dr Steve Peters: *The Chimp Paradox (2011), Ebury Publishing*

Mark Rashid: *Life Lessons from A Ranch Horse (2011); Skyhorse*

Matthew Syed: *Black Box Thinking; The Surprising Truth About Success (2015); John Murray.*

Glossary of terms

Below is a brief glossary of words or phrases that may be unfamiliar to non-riders, or those participating in different riding disciplines. And to any overseas readers.

Also-ran: A person who finished a very long way behind the winners. Usually used to mean unsuccessful or unimpressive performance.

Affiliated: A competition run under a national or international governing body. Different disciplines have their own governing bodies. Unaffiliated simply means competitions run outside these governance structures.

BE80 or BE90: Levels of competitions run by British Eventing. BE80 refers to events where the show-jumps and cross-country fences are no higher than 80cm. For BE90 they are capped at 90cm. Dressage tests are progressively more challenging as you move up the levels, as are the technical difficulties of the jumping challenges.

BHS: British Horse Society. The largest equestrian charity and membership organization in the UK. Has an educational structure which trains, examines and accredits riding instructors, and other equine professionals.

BHS Fellow: Someone who has been awarded the BHS Fellowship, widely considered the highest equestrian qualification in the world.

Black Flagged: On some cross-country courses, harder jumps can be black flagged, which means that the jump could be missed out in favour of a longer route to an easier fence. This would add time, so to avoid time penalties, it is always better to jump the 'direct' or the black flagged route.

Bottled it. British jargon for lost your nerve and/or pulled out of something due to nerves. 'I bottled the last jump, it just looked too big.'

CBT: Cognitive Behaviour Therapy. A Psychological Therapy focused on changing thoughts, feelings and behaviours, to relieve distress and improve functioning.

DBT: Dialectical Behaviour Therapy. A Psychological Therapy, developed for people with severe and unrelenting distress, who are at risk of hurting themselves or others. DBT includes a focus on gaining skills in emotional regulation and behavioural control.

Eventer Trial: A relaxed form of eventing, which usually only has the 2 jumping phases, and allows participants to treat the event like schooling round, in a competition environment. Eg competitors who are eliminated for refusals are not forced to stop jumping as soon as they are eliminated, but can continue, in order to give their horse experience.

Eventing: Taking part in competitions that involve dressage, show-jumping and cross-country over 1-3 days depending on the event.

Faff: British jargon to refer to wasting time with ineffectual or disorganized activity, as in 'faffing about'.

Farm Ride: A type of hack, common in the UK, that loops round private land, and is not generally accessible to vehicles, bikes etc. Often with optional jumps.

FEI: The International Federation for Equestrian Sports. The international governing body of equestrian sports.

Hack/Hacking: Riding outside an arena. Used as a noun or a verb. 'That was a lovely hack, I hacked through the forest for an hour, should we go hacking tomorrow.'

Happy Hacker: Someone who mainly rides trails and is generally uninterested in competing. Sometimes used pejoratively, often by the person themselves, who downplays the skill needed for trail riding. 'I'm *just* a happy hacker.'

Hobnobs: Popular chocolate-covered oat biscuit.

NHS: National Health Service. UK's nationwide health delivery service.

Novice (As related to eventing levels): Despite the name, Novice classes are big, bold and technical, strictly for very good horses and riders!

ODE: One Day Event. A competition comprising a dressage test, show-jumping round and cross-country course, all taking place on a single day.

3DE: A three day event in which the different elements of the event take place on separate days, usually ending with showjumping in reverse order.

Premier League: The highest football/soccer league in England and Wales.

Refusal: The horse stopping in front of the jump, instead of going over it.

Run out: The horse veering to the side of the jump, instead of going over it.

Stroppy: Informal British term for a person who is being unreasonably argumentative. Also a noun: 'She's in a strop.' Implies the person is struggling to cope.

Ultra-marathon or ultra: Any running distance further than a marathon, ie further than 26.2 miles or 42K. In practice, most races are not called ultras until they are 50K or more.

Wheels came off: British term for 'it all rapidly went wrong'.

Printed in Great Britain
by Amazon

20439223R00163